4th Grade

TEKS MATH TEST PREP

for

STAAR

INTRODUCTION

Our 4th Grade TEKS Math Test Prep for STAAR is an excellent resource to supplement your classroom's curriculum to assess and manage students' understanding of concepts outlined in the 2014-2015 TEKS STAAR Reporting Standards. This resource is divided into three sections: Diagnostic, Practice, and Assessment with multiple choice questions in each section. We recommend you use the Diagnostic section as a tool to determine the students' areas that need to be retaught. We also recommend you encourage your students to show their work to determine *how* and *why* the student arrived at an answer. The Practice section should be used to strengthen the students' knowledge by re-testing the standard to ensure comprehension of each standard. To ensure students' apply taught concepts in the classroom, we advise you use the Assessment section as a final test to verify the students' have mastered the standard.

This resource contains over 600 practice problems aligned to the 2014-2015 TEKS STAAR Reporting Standards. To view the reporting standards, refer to pages *i* through *v*.

Indicates the section of the book.

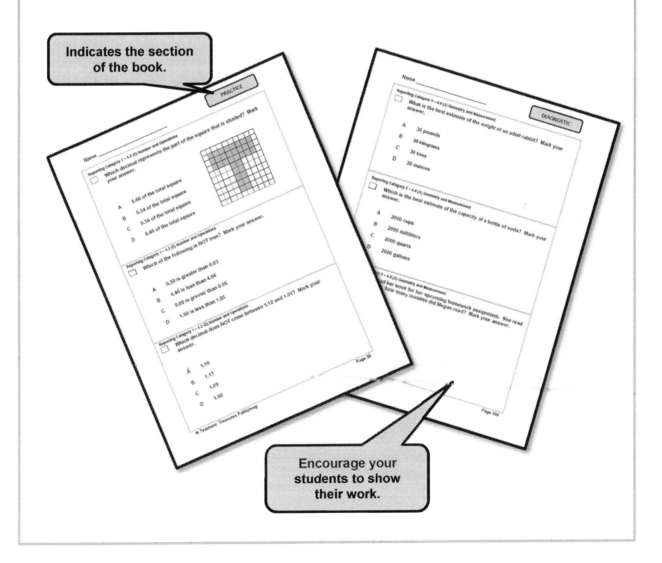

Encourage your students to show their work.

4th Grade
TEKS
Math Test Prep
FOR
STAAR

Reporting Category 1: Numerical Representations and Relationships

The student will demonstrate an understanding of how to represent and manipulate numbers and expressions.

(4.2) **Number and operations.** The student applies mathematical process standards to represent, compare, and order whole numbers and decimals and understand relationships related to place value. The student is expected to:

  (A) interpret the value of each place-value position as 10 times the position to the right and as one-tenth of the value of the place to its left; *Supporting Standard*

  (B) represent the value of the digit in whole numbers through 1,000,000,000 and decimals to the hundredths using expanded notation and numerals; *Readiness Standard*

  (C) compare and order whole numbers up to 1,000,000 and represent comparisons using the symbols >, <, or =; *Supporting Standard*

  (D) round whole numbers to a given place value through the hundred thousands place; *Supporting Standard*

  (E) represent decimals, including tenths and hundredths, using concrete and visual models and money; *Supporting Standard*

  (F) compare and order decimals using concrete and visual models to the hundredths; *Supporting Standard*

  (G) relate decimals to fractions that name tenths and hundredths; and *Readiness Standard*

  (H) determine the corresponding decimal to the tenths or hundredths place of a specified point on a number line. *Supporting Standard*

(4.3) **Number and operations.** The student applies mathematical process standards to represent and explain fractional units. The student is expected to:

  (A) represent a fraction *a / b* as a sum of fractions *1 / b,* where *a* and *b* are whole numbers and *b > 0*, including when *a > b*; *Supporting Standard*

  (B) decompose a fraction in more than one way into a sum of fractions with the same denominator using concrete and pictorial models and recording results with symbolic representations; *Supporting Standard*

  (C) determine if two given fractions are equivalent using a variety of methods; *Supporting Standard*

  (D) compare two fractions with different numerators and different denominators and represent the comparison using the symbols >, =, or <; and *Readiness Standard*

(E)   represent fractions and decimals to the tenths or hundredths as distances from zero on a number line.
Supporting Standard

Reporting Category 2: Computations and Algebraic Relationships

The student will demonstrate an understanding of how to perform operations and represent algebraic relationships.

(4.3) Number and operations. The student applies mathematical process standards to represent and generate fractions to solve problems. The student is expected to

(E)   represent and solve addition and subtraction of fractions with equal denominators using objects and pictorial models that build to the number line and properties of operations; and *Readiness Standard*

(F)   evaluate the reasonableness of sums and differences of fractions using benchmark fractions 0, 1/4, 1/2, 3/4, and 1, referring to the same whole.
Supporting Standard

(4.4)   Number and operations. The student applies mathematical process standards to develop and use strategies and methods for whole number computations and decimal sums and differences in order to solve problems with efficiency and accuracy. The student is expected to

(A)   add and subtract whole numbers and decimals to the hundredths place using the standard algorithm; *Readiness Standard*

(B)   determine products of a number and 10 or 100 using properties of operations and place value understandings;
Supporting Standard

(C)   represent the product of 2 two-digit numbers using arrays, area models, or equations, including perfect squares through 15 by 15; *Supporting Standard*

(D)   use strategies and algorithms, including the standard algorithm, to multiply up to a four-digit number by a one-digit number and to multiply a two-digit number by a two-digit number. Strategies may include mental math, partial products, and the commutative, associative, and distributive properties; *Supporting Standard*

(E)   represent the quotient of up to a four-digit whole number divided by a one-digit whole number using arrays, area models, or equations;
Supporting Standard

(F)   use strategies and algorithms, including the standard algorithm, to divide up to a four-digit dividend by a one-digit divisor; *Supporting Standard*

(G) round to the nearest 10, 100, or 1,000 or use compatible numbers to estimate solutions involving whole numbers; and
Supporting Standard

(H) solve with fluency one- and two-step problems involving multiplication and division, including interpreting remainders.
Readiness Standard

(4.5) Algebraic reasoning. The student applies mathematical process standards to develop concepts of expressions and equations. The student is expected to

(A) represent multi-step problems involving the four operations with whole numbers using strip diagrams and equations with a letter standing for the unknown quantity; and
Readiness Standard

(B) represent problems using an input-output table and numerical expressions to generate a number pattern that follows a given rule representing the relationship of the values in the resulting sequence and their position in the sequence.
Readiness Standard

Reporting Category 3: Geometry and Measurement

The student will demonstrate an understanding of how to represent and apply geometry and measurement concepts.

(4.5) **Algebraic reasoning.** The student applies mathematical process standards to develop concepts of expressions and equations. The student is expected to

   (D)   solve problems related to perimeter and area of rectangles where dimensions are whole numbers.
   Readiness Standard

(4.6) **Geometry and measurement.** The student applies mathematical process standards to analyze geometric attributes in order to develop generalizations about their properties. The student is expected to

   (A)   identify points, lines, line segments, rays, angles, and perpendicular and parallel lines; *Supporting Standard*
   (B)   identify and draw one or more lines of symmetry, if they exist, for a two-dimensional figure; *Supporting Standard*
   (C)   apply knowledge of right angles to identify acute, right, and obtuse triangles; and *Supporting Standard*
   (D)   classify two-dimensional figures based on the presence or absence of parallel or perpendicular lines or the presence or absence of angles of a specified size. *Readiness Standard*

(4.7) **Geometry and measurement.** The student applies mathematical process standards to solve problems involving angles less than or equal to 180 degrees. The student is expected to

   (C)   determine the approximate measures of angles in degrees to the nearest whole number using a protractor; *Readiness Standard*
   (D)   draw an angle with a given measure; and *Supporting Standard*
   (E)   determine the measure of an unknown angle formed by two non-overlapping adjacent angles given one or both angle measures. *Supporting Standard*

(4.8) **Geometry and measurement.** The student applies mathematical process standards to select appropriate customary and metric units, strategies, and tools to solve problems involving measurement. The student is expected to

    (A)   identify relative sizes of measurement units within the customary and metric systems; *Supporting Standard*

    (B)   convert measurements within the same measurement system, customary or metric, from a smaller unit into a larger unit or a larger unit into a smaller unit when given other equivalent measures represented in a table; and *Supporting Standard*

    (C)   solve problems that deal with measurements of length, intervals of time, liquid volumes, mass, and money using addition, subtraction, multiplication, or division as appropriate. *Readiness Standard*

Reporting Category 4: Data Analysis and Personal Financial Literacy

The student will demonstrate an understanding of how to represent and analyze data and how to describe and apply personal financial concepts.

(4.9) **Data analysis.** The student applies mathematical process standards to solve problems by collecting, organizing, displaying, and interpreting data. The student is expected to

    (A)   represent data on a frequency table, dot plot, or stem-and-leaf plot marked with whole numbers and fractions; and *Readiness Standard*

    (B)   solve one- and two-step problems using data in whole number, decimal, and fraction form in a frequency table, dot plot, or stem- and-leaf plot. *Supporting Standard*

Name _____

Reporting Category 1 – 4.2 (A) Number and Operations

☐ Which choice has a digit in the ones place that is exactly five times the value of the digit in the tens place? Mark your answer.

   A   642

   B   515

   C   341

   D   551

Reporting Category 1 – 4.2 (A) Number and Operations

☐ Which choice has a digit in the tens place that is exactly eight times the value of the digit in the ones place? Mark your answer.

   A   91

   B   81

   C   35

   D   104

Reporting Category 1 – 4.2 (A) Number and Operations

☐ Which choice has a digit in the hundred thousands place that is exactly twice the value of the digit in the millions place? Mark your answer.

   A   1,354,148

   B   2,441,224

   C   6,749,799

   D   8,372,991

Reporting Category 1 – 4.2 (A) Number and Operations

☐ **Which choice has a digit in the ten thousands place that is exactly twice the value of the digit in the tens place? Mark your answer.**

A   1,165,937

B   341,461

C   33,661

D   661,129

Reporting Category 1 – 4.2 (A) Number and Operations

☐ **Which choice has a digit in the ten thousands place that is exactly twice the value of the digit in the hundreds place? Mark your answer.**

A   914,514

B   782,411

C   514,102

D   222,427

Reporting Category 1 – 4.2 (A) Number and Operations

☐ **Which choice has a digit in the hundreds place that is exactly three times the value of the digit in the ten thousands place? Mark your answer.**

A   592,478

B   824,117

C   928,613

D   324,842

Reporting Category 1 – 4.2 (A) Number and Operations

☐ **Which choice has a digit in the thousands place that is exactly nine times the value of the digit in the tens place? Mark your answer.**

A   99,551

B   89,502

C   78,554

D   79,213

Reporting Category 1 – 4.2 (A) Number and Operations

☐ **Which choice has a digit in the hundreds place that is exactly four times the value of the digit in the tens place? Mark your answer.**

A   826

B   846

C   315

D   981

Reporting Category 1 – 4.2 (A) Number and Operations

☐ **Which choice has a digit in the ones place that is exactly five times the value of the digit in the thousands place? Mark your answer.**

A   3,157

B   2,114

C   1,345

D   3,115

Reporting Category 1 – 4.2 (A) Number and Operations

[ ] **Which choice has a digit in the ones place that is exactly four times the value of the digit in the tens place? Mark your answer.**

A   77,651

B   938,728

C   1,715

D   22,148

Reporting Category 1 – 4.2 (A) Number and Operations

[ ] **Which choice has a digit in the tens thousands place that is exactly three times the value of the digit in the tens place? Mark your answer.**

A   7,164,421

B   5,342,978

C   46,854

D   9,481,352

Reporting Category 1 – 4.2 (A) Number and Operations

[ ] **Which choice has a digit in the hundreds place that is exactly three times the value of the digit in the thousands place? Mark your answer.**

A   621,543

B   875,728

C   131,359

D   234,822

Name _____

Reporting Category 1 – 4.2 (B) Number and Operations

☐ **Which number has a 6 in the ten thousands place and a 4 in the hundreds place? Mark your answer.**

A   1,463,491

B   6,463,941

C   1,636,491

D   4,636,149

Reporting Category 1 – 4.2 (B) Number and Operations

☐ **The Superdome in New Orleans has a total floor area of 82,342 square meters. How is this number of square meters written in words? Mark your answer.**

A   Eighty-two ten thousand, three hundred forty-two

B   Eighty-two, three hundred forty-two

C   Eight two thousand, three forty-two

D   Eighty-two thousand, three hundred forty-two

Reporting Category 1 – 4.2 (B) Number and Operations

☐ **Which of the following is equal to 271,049? Mark your answer.**

A   200,000 + 70,000 + 1,000 + 100 + 40 + 9

B   200,000 + 70,000 + 1,000 + 40 + 9

C   2,000,000 + 700,000 + 10,000 + 400 + 9

D   2 + 7 + 1 + 0 + 4 + 9

Reporting Category 1 – 4.2 (B) Number and Operations

☐ **Which of the following is equal to 100,000 + 5,000 + 300 + 90? Mark your answer.**

A   153,900

B   105,309

C   1,539

D   105,390

Reporting Category 1 – 4.2 (B) Number and Operations

☐ **What is the value of the 8 in 8,502,734? Mark your answer.**

A   8 thousand

B   8 hundred thousand

C   8 million

D   8 hundred million

Reporting Category 1 – 4.2 (B) Number and Operations

☐ **The population of Louisiana in 2000 was four million, four hundred sixty-eight thousand, nine hundred seventy-six. How is this number written? Mark your answer.**

A   40,468,976

B   4,468,976

C   400,468,976

D   4,468,967

Name _____

Reporting Category 1 – 4.2 (B) Number and Operations

☐ **Which number has a 9 in the hundreds place? Mark your answer.**

A   469,207

B   358,927

C   120,493

D   893,528

Reporting Category 1 – 4.2 (B) Number and Operations

☐ **Jerome and his brother played a game while they waited for their mother. They each wrote six numbers on a piece of paper, circled one of the numbers, and then exchanged the pieces of paper. Each boy had to make the largest number possible using all of the numbers and place the circled number in the thousands place. What is the largest number Jerome could have made if he used the numbers 9, 4, 6, 3, 7, 1, and the 4 was circled? Mark your answer.**

A   974,631   C   134,679

B   947,631   D   976,431

Reporting Category 1 – 4.2 (B) Number and Operations

☐ **Which number has an 8 in the thousands place and a 6 in the ones place? Mark your answer.**

A   483,566

B   637,586

C   528,616

D   738,862

Reporting Category 1 – 4.2 (B) Number and Operations

☐ The area of Guinea is 94,964 square miles. How would this area be written in words? Mark your answer.

A   Nine thousand four, nine hundred six and four

B   Ninety-four, nine hundred sixty-four

C   Ninety-four thousand, nine hundred sixty-four

D   Nine hundred four thousand, nine hundred sixty-four

Reporting Category 1 – 4.2 (B) Number and Operations

☐ Which of the following is equal to 1,570,339? Mark your answer.

A   1,000,000 + 500,000 + 70,000 + 3,000 + 30 + 9

B   1 + 5 + 7 + 3 + 3 + 9

C   1,000,000 + 500 + 70 + 300 + 39

D   1,000,000 + 500,000 + 70,000 + 300 + 30 + 9

Reporting Category 1 – 4.2 (B) Number and Operations

☐ Which of the following is equal to 1,000,000 + 3,000 + 500 + 40 + 2? Mark your answer.

A   1,003,542

B   1,354,200

C   1,300,542

D   1,035,420

Reporting Category 1 – 4.2 (B) Number and Operations

☐ **What is the place value of the 6 in 3,670,209? Mark your answer.**

A   6 hundred thousands

B   6 thousands

C   6 millions

D   6 ten thousands

Reporting Category 1 – 4.2 (B) Number and Operations

☐ **When the University of Texas Longhorns won the national championship in football in 2005, a web site sold five hundred thirty-seven thousand, nine hundred eighteen Longhorn T-shirts in one day. How is this number of T-shirts written? Mark your answer.**

A   5,370, 918

B   5,003,798

C   537,980

D   537,918

Reporting Category 1 – 4.2 (B) Number and Operations

☐ **Which number has a 7 in the ten thousands place? Mark your answer.**

A   367,201

B   2,405,799

C   970,463

D   728,458

Reporting Category 1 – 4.2 (B) Number and Operations

☐ A local TV station sponsored a contest for fourth grade students. The students had to make as many numbers as they could using the following numbers: 8, 5, 1, 9, 0, 2, and 7. They were to begin with the largest number possible and end with the smallest number. However, each number had to use the 2 in the hundred thousands place. What number should each child's entry begin with? Mark your answer.

A   9,827,510

B   9,278,510

C   9,287,510

D   2,872,510

Reporting Category 1 – 4.2 (B) Number and Operations

☐ Which number has a 4 in the ten thousands place and a 5 in the hundred thousands place? Mark your answer.

A   5,424,501

B   6,534,354

C   5,745,365

D   3,543,459

Reporting Category 1 – 4.2 (B) Number and Operations

☐ What is the place value of the 3 in 538,091? Mark your answer.

A   Hundred thousands

B   Ten thousands

C   Thousands

D   Millions

Reporting Category 1 – 4.2 (B) Number and Operations

☐ **What is the place value of the 8 in 8,030,274? Mark your answer.**

A   **Millions**

B   **Hundred thousands**

C   **Hundred millions**

D   **Ten thousands**

Reporting Category 1 – 4.2 (B) Number and Operations

☐ **Which of the following is equal to 1,000,000 + 300,000 + 40,000 + 2,000 + 70? Mark your answer.**

A   **1,300,427**

B   **1,342,070**

C   **1,340,270**

D   **1,342,700**

Reporting Category 1 – 4.2 (B) Number and Operations

☐ **In 2000 there were 880,047 people with a disability living in Texas. How is this number written in words? Mark your answer.**

A   **Eight hundred eighty, forty-seven**

B   **Eight thousand eighty, forty-seven**

C   **Eight hundred eighty thousand, forty-seven**

D   **Eight hundred eighty thousand, four hundred seven**

Reporting Category 1 – 4.2 (B) Number and Operations

☐ **Which of the following is equal to 1,580,006? Mark your answer.**

A   1,000,000 + 500,000 + 80,000 + 600

B   1,000,000 + 500,000 + 8,000 + 6

C   1,000,000 + 500,000 + 80,000 + 6

D   1 + 5 + 8 + 6

Reporting Category 1 – 4.2 (B) Number and Operations

☐ **What is the place value of the 7 in 1,742,081? Mark your answer.**

A   Thousands

B   Millions

C   Hundred ten thousands

D   Hundred thousands

Reporting Category 1 – 4.2 (B) Number and Operations

☐ **What is the value of the 4 in 842,093? Mark your answer.**

A   4 thousands

B   4 ten thousands

C   4 millions

D   4 hundred thousands

Name _____

Reporting Category 1 – 4.2 (C) Number and Operations

☐ **Which group of numbers is in order from *greatest* to *least*? Mark your answer.**

A   1,637,537   1,636, 419   1,637,020   1,636,342

B   1,637,537   1,637,020   1,636,419   1,636,342

C   1,636,342   1,636,419   1,637,020   1,637,537

D   1,637,537   1,637,020   1,636,342   1,636,419

Reporting Category 1 – 4.2 (C) Number and Operations

☐ **Which numeral has a larger digit in the hundreds place than in the tens place? Mark your answer.**

A   356,281

B   1,375,290

C   27,192

D   6,437

Reporting Category 1 – 4.2 (C) Number and Operations

☐ **Which group of numbers is in order from *least* to *greatest*? Mark your answer.**

A   535,743   535,410   535,088   534,874

B   534,874   535,088   535,410   535,743

C   534,874   535,088   535,743   535,410

D   535,743   535,088   535,410   534,874

Reporting Category 1 – 4.2 (C) Number and Operations

☐ **Which statement is true? Mark your answer.**

A   4,257,138 > 4,257,039

B   2,429,236 > 2,429,238

C   1,478,533 < 1,478,532

D   3,305,131 > 3,305,135

Reporting Category 1 – 4.2 (C) Number and Operations

☐ **A movie theater kept a record of the number of tickets they sold. In January they sold 5,390 tickets, 5,178 tickets in February, 5,199 tickets in March, and 5,096 tickets in April. Which shows the number of tickets sold in order from *greatest* to *least*? Mark your answer.**

A   5,390   5,096   5,178   5,199

B   5,096   5,178   5,199   5,390

C   5,390   5,199   5,178   5,096

D   5,390   5,178   5,199   5,096

Reporting Category 1 – 4.2 (C) Number and Operations

☐ **It is time for school pictures. The students must line up in order from the tallest to the shortest. April is 48 inches tall, Brad is 56 inches tall, Callie is 50 inches tall, and David is 55 inches tall. In which order should the students line up? Mark your answer.**

A   Brad, April, Callie, David

B   April, Callie, David, Brad

C   April, Brad, Callie, David

D   Brad, David, Callie, April

Height of Students

Student	Height in Inches
April	48 in
Brad	56 in
Callie	50 in
David	55 in

Reporting Category 1 – 4.2 (C) Number and Operations

☐ **Which numeral has a larger digit in the hundreds place than in the thousands place? Mark your answer.**

A   500,005

B   133,256

C   750,682

D   352,110

Reporting Category 1 – 4.2 (C) Number and Operations

☐ **Which group of numbers is in order from *least* to *greatest*? Mark your answer.**

A   849,039   849,752   849,849   849,982

B   849,039   849,849   849,752   849,982

C   849,982   849,849   849,752   849,039

D   849,039   849,752   849,982   849,849

Reporting Category 1 – 4.2 (C) Number and Operations

☐ **Which statement is true? Mark your answer.**

A   731 < 146 + 29

B   410 > 510

C   154 − 41 < 98

D   819 = 800 + 19

Name ___________________________

PRACTICE

Reporting Category 1 – 4.2 (C) Number and Operations

☐ Jared's dad sells used cars. On his used car lot he has a Chevrolet that has been driven 134,890 miles, an Oldsmobile that has been driven 145,201, a Buick that has been driven 134,809 miles, and a Toyota that has been driven 142,328 miles. Which shows the number of miles the cars have been driven in order from *greatest* to *least*? Mark your answer.

A	145,201	142,328	134,890	134,809
B	142,328	145,201	134,809	134,890
C	145,201	142,328	134,809	134,890
D	134,809	134,890	142,328	145,201

Reporting Category 1 – 4.2 (C) Number and Operations

☐ The Farmer Dairy Company has kept a record of sales for every ten years. The sales were $168,499 in 2004; $180,982 in 1994; $120,001 in 1984; and $108,955 in 1974. If the sales totals are put in order from the worst year to the best year, which order would be correct? Mark your answer.

Sales

Year	Sales in Dollars
2004	$168,499
1994	$180,982
1984	$120,001
1974	$108,955

A	$168,499	$180,982	$120,001	$108,955
B	$180,982	$168,499	$120,001	$108,955
C	$108,955	$120,001	$168,499	$180,982
D	$108,955	$168,499	$120,001	$180,982

Reporting Category 1 – 4.2 (C) Number and Operations

☐ Which group of numbers is in order from *greatest* to *least*? Mark your answer.

A	3,744,560	3,744,428	3,744,508	3,744,499
B	3,744,428	3,744,499	3,744,508	3,744,560
C	3,744,560	3,744,508	3,744,428	3,744,499
D	3,744,560	3,744,508	3,744,499	3,744,428

Reporting Category 1 – 4.2 (C) Number and Operations

☐ **Which group of numbers is in order from *least* to *greatest*? Mark your answer.**

A   4,730,017   4,730,100   4,730,193   4,730,001

B   4,730,001   4,730,100   4,730,193   4,730,017

C   4,730,001   4,730,017   4,730,100   4,730,193

D   4,730,193   4,730,100   4,730,017   4,730,001

Reporting Category 1 – 4.2 (C) Number and Operations

☐ **Which statement is true? Mark your answer.**

A $36 \div 4 < 72 \div 9$

B $140 \div 14 = (10 \times 12) \div 12$

C $84 \div 7 > 13 \times 3$

D $8 \times 15 < 1000 \div 20$

Reporting Category 1 – 4.2 (C) Number and Operations

☐ **Mr. Jackson's class is learning about a small country in South America. For several years the country's population has increased and decreased. In 1990 the population was 347,580, and in 1992 it was 336,977. In 1994 the population was 347,008, and in 1996 it was 347,500. If the students put the population numbers in order from *greatest* to *least*, which order would they chose? Mark your answer.**

A   347,580   347,008   347,500   336,977

B   336,977   347,008   347,500   347,580

C   347,500   347,580   347,008   336,977

D   347,580   347,500   347,008   336,977

Reporting Category 1 – 4.2 (C) Number and Operations

☐ A city in Texas listed its population figures for four years. If the figures are arranged in order from the smallest number of people to the largest number of people, which order of years would be correct? Mark your answer.

A	2002	2003	2001	2004
B	2002	2003	2004	2001
C	2001	2004	2003	2002
D	2003	2004	2001	2002

Year	Population
2001	327,580
2002	326,977
2003	327,009
2004	327,050

Reporting Category 1 – 4.2 (C) Number and Operations

☐ Which group of numbers is in order from *greatest* to *least*? Mark your answer.

A	2,452,201	2,452,225	2,452,261	2,452,319
B	2,452,261	2,452,225	2,452,319	2,452,201
C	2,452,319	2,452,261	2,452,225	2,452,201
D	2,452,319	2,452,225	2,452,261	2,452,201

Reporting Category 1 – 4.2 (C) Number and Operations

☐ Which numeral has a larger digit in the thousands place than in the millions place? Mark your answer.

A   1,547,293

B   3,652,018

C   5,324,000

D   1,201,538

Name _____

Reporting Category 1 – 4.2 (D) Number and Operations

☐ Luis counted the number of cars on school parking lots. There were 116 cars parked at the elementary school and 259 cars parked on the high school parking lot. About how many cars did he count altogether? Mark your answer.

A   200

B   300

C   100

D   400

Reporting Category 1 – 4.2 (D) Number and Operations

☐ Abigail bought a set of video games on sale. She paid $27 for the games. The suggested retail price of the set of video games was from $49 to $55. Which could be the amount Lacey saved by buying the games on sale rather than paying the suggested retail price? Mark your answer.

A $5

B $40

C $10

D $20

Reporting Category 1 – 4.2 (D) Number and Operations

☐ Nathan's score on a video game was 3,752. What is his score rounded to the nearest hundred? Mark your answer

A   3,700

B   3,750

C   3,800

D   4,000

Reporting Category 1 – 4.2 (D) Number and Operations

☐ Kevin wanted to buy a shirt that cost $14.79, a pair of slacks that cost $29.50, and some socks that cost $6.99. *About* how much will he spend for the three items? Mark your answer.

A $45

B $50

C $52

D $47

Reporting Category 1 – 4.2 (D) Number and Operations

☐ The table below shows the number of books sold in 5 different countries.

Country	Number of Books
France	2,497
Australia	1,046
Mexico	3,217
China	2,904
Canada	1,610

Which 3 countries combined number of books sold is about 7,000? Mark your answer.

A   France, Australia, and China

B   Canada, Australia, and Mexico

C   China, Mexico, and France

D   Australia, Canada, and Mexico

Reporting Category 1 – 4.2 (D) Number and Operations

☐ **Grace, Mackenzie, and Chloe went to lunch together last Saturday. Grace's bill was $5.25, Chloe's bill was $5.49, and Mackenzie's lunch cost $4.95. About how much did they spend altogether for lunch? Mark your answer.**

A $15

B $20

C $17

D $14

Reporting Category 1 – 4.2 (D) Number and Operations

☐ **Mr. Sanger bought an HD television from a friend who was moving to Italy. The television would have cost between $1250 and $1500 if he had bought it new. If Mr. Sanger paid his friend $520 for the television, which could be the amount he saved by buying it from his friend rather than buying a new television? Mark your answer.**

A $1100

B $500

C $1000

D $700

Reporting Category 1 – 4.2 (D) Number and Operations

☐ **The table below shows the total number of fourth grade students enrolled in 5 intermediate schools. Which schools have a combined fourth grade enrollment of about 2,000 students? Mark your answer.**

A   **Madison and Riverside**

B   **Riverside, Butler, and Tuttle**

C   **Butler and Saddle Brook**

D   **Tuttle, Saddle Brook, and Butler**

Name of School	Number of Students
Butler Int.	542
Saddle Brook Int.	721
Madison Int.	1,550
Tuttle Int.	928
Riverside Int.	1,006

Reporting Category 1 – 4.2 (D) Number and Operations

☐ Connor's family traveled 1,559 miles on their vacation. What is their mileage rounded to the nearest hundred? Mark your answer.

A 2,000 mi

B 1,560 mi

C 1,500 mi

D 1,600 mi

Reporting Category 1 – 4.2 (D) Number and Operations

☐ Demetrius brought $5 for lunch. Which of the choices below represent what he can purchase and not spend more than $5? Mark your answer.

Lunch Menu	
Soup	$2.99
Sandwiches	
Chicken	$3.99
Ham & Cheese	$4.75
Turkey	$3.50
Tuna Salad	$2.30
Drinks	
Cola	$1.25
Bottled Tea	$2.75
Bottled Water	$0.95

A Ham & cheese sandwich and water

B Soup and bottled tea

C Turkey sandwich and cola

D Chicken sandwich and bottled tea

Reporting Category 1 – 4.2 (D) Number and Operations

☐ Lily's reading goal was 3,800 pages. One six weeks she read 956 pages. The next six weeks she read 1,127 pages. *About* how many more pages does she need to read to reach her goal? Mark your answer.

A 2,000

B 200

C 1,400

D 1,700

Reporting Category 1 – 4.2 (D) Number and Operations

☐ Mrs. Miller made curtains and a bedspread for her bedroom. She used 33 yards of fabric to make the items. She made curtains and bedspreads for the other bedrooms in her house and used between 44 and 51 yards of fabric. Which could be how much less fabric Mrs. Miller used on the curtains for her bedroom than the fabric used for the other bedrooms? Mark your answer.

A 5 yards

B 10 yards

C 30 yards

D 40 yards

Reporting Category 1 – 4.2 (D) Number and Operations

☐ Eli's brother wants to sell his truck. He advertised it in a newspaper for $7,067. What is the price of the truck rounded to the nearest hundred? Mark your answer.

A $7,100

B $7,070

C $7,000

D $8,000

Reporting Category 1 – 4.2 (D) Number and Operations

☐ Lauren added 1,468 and 3,704. Which could be an estimate of the total? Mark your answer.

A   6,000

B   5,200

C   5,100

D   3,000

Reporting Category 1 – 4.2 (D) Number and Operations

☐ The table below shows the number of viewers of six o'clock news programs for 5 local TV channels.

TV Station	Number of Viewers
Channel 12	974
Channel 7	1,900
Channel 6	2,829
Channel 10	2,948
Channel 2	1,374

Which 3 stations have a combined number of viewers of about 8,000? Mark your answer.

A   Channels 6, 7, and 10

B   Channels 2, 6, and 12

C   Channels 2, 6, and 10

D   Channels 6, 10, and 12

Name _____

Reporting Category 1 – 4.2 (D) Number and Operations

☐ The table below shows the area in kilometers of 4 countries. Which is the best estimate of how much larger Cape Verde is than Luxembourg? Mark your answer.

Country	Area
Luxembourg	2,586
Trinidad	5,128
Samoa	2,831
Cape Verde	4,033

A   2,000 km

B   1,000 km

C   3,000 km

D   100 km

Reporting Category 1 – 4.2 (D) Number and Operations

☐ Sofia mixed 1.7 liters of red paint, 2.3 liters of white paint, and 1.3 liters of green paint. About how many liters of paint did Sofia make? Mark your answer.

A   6

B   7

C   4

D   5

Reporting Category 1 – 4.2 (D) Number and Operations

☐ There were 2,605 projects at a science fair. The judges viewed 478 on the first day and 720 on the second day of the fair. About how many more projects need to be viewed by the judges? Mark your answer.

A   1,000

B   2,000

C   1,500

D   1,400

Reporting Category 1 – 4.2 (D) Number and Operations

☐   Ms. Moses bought a new dining room suite for $4,512. What is the price of the dining room suite rounded to the nearest hundred?   Mark your answer.

A $5,000

B $4,500

C $4,000

D $4,510

Reporting Category 1 – 4.2 (D) Number and Operations

☐   The table below shows the length of some rivers found in North America.

River	Length (in kilometers)
Snake River	1,670 km
Missouri River	3,725 km
Brazos River	1,485 km
Mississippi River	3,778 km
Rio Grande River	2,840 km

Which 3 rivers have a combined length of about 6,000 kilometers? Mark your answer.

A   Snake, Mississippi, and Rio Grande Rivers

B   Snake, Brazos, and Mississippi Rivers

C   Brazos, Snake, and Rio Grande Rivers

D   Mississippi, Rio Grande, and Missouri Rivers

Reporting Category 1 – 4.2 (E) Number and Operations

☐ **Which of the following is true? Mark your answer.**

A   0.03 is greater than 0.24

B   0.48 is less than 0.84

C   0.7 is greater than 0.74

D   0.88 is less than 0.8

Reporting Category 1 – 4.2 (E) Number and Operations

☐ **Which of the following is the same as 4 hundredths? Mark your answer.**

A   0.04

B   0.4

C   0.40

D   4.00

Reporting Category 1 – 4.2 (E) Number and Operations

☐ **Which decimal comes between 0.4 and 0.5? Mark your answer.**

A   0.40

B   0.50

C   0.45

D   0.55

Reporting Category 1 – 4.2 (E) Number and Operations

☐ If three more balls are shaded, which decimal represents the total number of shaded balls? Mark your answer.

A   0.5

B   0.3

C   0.7

D   0.07

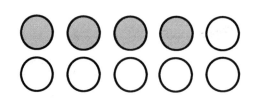

Reporting Category 1 – 4.2 (E) Number and Operations

☐ Which decimal represents the shaded part of the figure? Mark your answer.

A   0.03

B   0.3

C   0.7

D   0.37

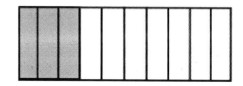

Reporting Category 1 – 4.2 (E) Number and Operations

☐ Mrs. Floyd bought a new rug. Which decimal shows how much of her new rug is made up of squares with stripes? Mark your answer.

A   0.40 of the total rug

B   0.38 of the total rug

C   0.36 of the total rug

D   0.30 of the total rug

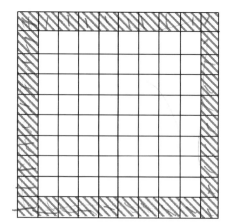

Reporting Category 1 – 4.2 (E) Number and Operations

☐ **Three of the T-shirts have designs. How would that amount be written in decimal form? Mark your answer.**

A   0.03

B   10.3

C   3.0

D   0.3

Reporting Category 1 – 4.2 (E) Number and Operations

☐ **Which of the following is the same as 4 tenths? Mark your answer.**

A   0.4

B   0.04

C   4.0

D   0.004

Reporting Category 1 – 4.2 (E) Number and Operations

☐ **If Caleb colors three more kites, which decimal represents the number of colored kites? Mark your answer.**

A   0.3

B   0.6

C   0.9

D   0.4

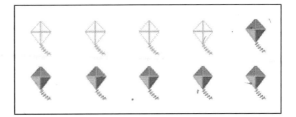

Reporting Category 1 – 4.2 (E) Number and Operations

☐ **Which decimal represents the part of the square that is shaded? Mark your answer.**

A   0.66 of the total square

B   0.34 of the total square

C   0.36 of the total square

D   0.46 of the total square

Reporting Category 1 – 4.2 (E) Number and Operations

☐ **Which of the following is NOT true? Mark your answer.**

A   0.30 is greater than 0.03

B   4.40 is less than 4.04

C   0.09 is greater than 0.06

D   1.00 is less than 1.85

Reporting Category 1 – 4.2 (E) Number and Operations

☐ **Which decimal does NOT come between 1.12 and 1.01? Mark your answer.**

A   1.10

B   1.11

C   1.09

D   1.00

Reporting Category 1 – 4.2 (E) Number and Operations

☐   **Which decimal comes between 1.02 and 0.99? Mark your answer.**

A   0.98

B   1.05

C   0.89

D   1.00

Reporting Category 1 – 4.2 (E) Number and Operations

☐   **Which of the following is the same as 5 hundredths? Mark your answer.**

A   5.00

B   0.5

C   0.05

D   0.50

Reporting Category 1 – 4.2 (E) Number and Operations

☐   **Which shaded figure below represents the decimal 0.75? Mark your answer.**

A

C

B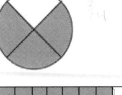

D

Reporting Category 1 – 4.2 (E) Number and Operations

Max wants to draw 10 snakes. If he draws two more snakes, which decimal represents the number of snakes he will have drawn so far? Mark your answer.

A   0.6

B   0.04

C   0.06

D   0.4

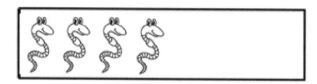

Reporting Category 1 – 4.2 (E) Number and Operations

Which of the following is true? Mark your answer.

A   0.01 is greater than 0.03

B   2.54 is less than 2.45

C   0.06 is greater than 0.60

D   1.02 is less than 1.20

Reporting Category 1 – 4.2 (E) Number and Operations

Which decimal represents the part of the square that is not shaded? Mark your answer.

A   0.25 of the total square

B   0.85 of the total square

C   0.22 of the total square

D   0.75 of the total square

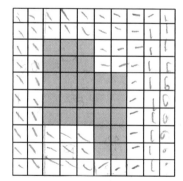

Reporting Category 1 – 4.2 (E) Number and Operations

☐ **Which of the following is NOT true? Mark your answer.**

A   0.34 is greater than 0.034

B   0.10 is less than 0.01

C   0.17 is less than 1.7

D   2.0 is greater than 0.20

Reporting Category 1 – 4.2 (E) Number and Operations

☐ **Which of the following is the same as 3 hundredths? Mark your answer.**

A   3.0

B   0.3

C   0.300

D   0.03

Reporting Category 1 – 4.2 (E) Number and Operations

☐ **Which decimal represents the unshaded part of the figure? Mark your answer.**

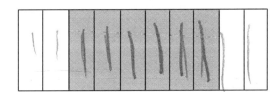

A   0.6

B   0.06

C   0.4

D   0.04

Reporting Category 1 – 4.2 (E) Number and Operations

Which decimal does NOT come between 0.02 and 0.20? Mark your answer.

     A   0.10

     B   0.19

     C   0.04

     D   0.01

Reporting Category 1 – 4.2 (E) Number and Operations

If Mrs. Miller places 4 more teddy bears in the box, which decimal represents the total number of teddy bears? Mark your answer.

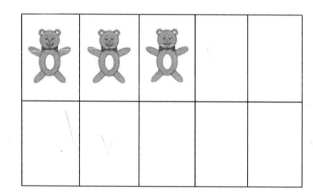

     A   0.7

     B   0.4

     C   0.07

     D   7.0

Reporting Category 1 – 4.2 (E) Number and Operations

Which decimal represents the part of the square that is not shaded? Mark your answer.

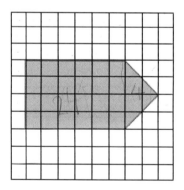

     A   0.26 of the total square

     B   0.82 of the total square

     C   0.28 of the total square

     D   0.72 of the total square

Reporting Category 1 – 4.2 (F) Number and Operations

☐   **Martin has $.70. How much money does he have? Mark your answer.**

A   Two quarters and two dimes

B   Three quarters and one nickel

C   Seven nickels

D   One quarter, three dimes, and one nickel

Reporting Category 1 – 4.2 (F) Number and Operations

☐   **If Kathryn brought 3 five dollar bills, 1 quarter, and 4 nickels to school, how much money did she bring? Mark your answer.**

A $15.65

B $35.14

C $3.45

D $15.45

Reporting Category 1 – 4.2 (F) Number and Operations

☐   **Which group of coins is in order from *greatest to least*? Mark your answer.**

A

B

C

D

Reporting Category 1 – 4.2 (F) Number and Operations

☐ **Felix gave his sister $.54 to buy a pencil. How much money did he give his sister? Mark your answer.**

A One quarter, two dimes, one nickel, and 4 pennies

B Five dimes and one nickel

C Five nickels and 4 pennies

D Two dimes, five nickels, and 4 pennies

Reporting Category 1 – 4.2 (F) Number and Operations

☐ **McKenna brought one dollar bill, four quarters, one dime, and three nickels to school to buy a book during the library book fair. How much money did she bring? Mark your answer.**

A $1.95

B $2.35

C $2.25

D $14.13

Reporting Category 1 – 4.2 (F) Number and Operations

☐ **Which of the following does NOT equal $1.35? Mark your answer.**

A 5 quarters, 2 nickels

B 6 quarters, 1 dime

C 4 quarters, 3 dimes, 1 nickel

D 13 dimes, 1 nickel

Reporting Category 1 – 4.2 (F) Number and Operations

☐   **Which of the following equals $3.04?**

A   **3 one dollar bills, 4 dimes**

B   **3 one dollar bills, 4 nickels**

C   **2 one dollar bills, 4 quarters, 4 pennies**

D   **1 dollar bill, 6 quarters, 6 dimes, 4 pennies**

Reporting Category 1 – 4.2 (F) Number and Operations

☐   **Wyatt spent $1.35 for a package of balloons. How much money did he spend? Mark your answer.**

A   **One dollar and one quarter**

B   **Four quarters, one dime and three nickels**

C   **One dollar, two dimes, and two nickels**

D   **Four quarters, three dimes, and five pennies**

Reporting Category 1 – 4.2 (F) Number and Operations

☐   **Mr. David's class contributed 4 one dollar bills, 12 dimes, 11 pennies, and 3 quarters to a fund to buy feed for the class hamster. How much money did the students contribute? Mark your answer.**

A   **$6.06**

B   **$30.00**

C   **$4.26**

D   **$2.10**

Reporting Category 1 – 4.2 (F) Number and Operations

☐ **Which of the following does NOT equal $1.01? Mark your answer.**

A   3 quarters, 2 dimes, 1 nickel, 1 penny

B   8 dimes, 4 nickels, 1 penny

C   4 quarters, 1 dime

D   12 nickels, 4 dimes, 1 penny

Reporting Category 1 – 4.2 (F) Number and Operations

☐ **Juan saved 3 one dollar bills, 4 half dollars, 2 quarters, and 4 nickels. How much money did he save? Mark your answer.**

A $13.00

B $5.70

C $5.20

D $4.80

Reporting Category 1 – 4.2 (F) Number and Operations

☐ **Allison has $1.48. How much money does she have? Mark your answer.**

A   Five quarters, 2 dimes, 3 pennies

B   Five quarters, 2 nickels, 3 pennies

C   Four quarters, 5 nickels, 3 pennies

D   Four quarters, 8 nickels, 3 pennies

Name _____

☐ Jonathan played 10 computer games and won 6 of the games or 0.6 when written as a decimal. Which fraction shows the number of games he won? Mark your answer.

A $\frac{4}{10}$

B $\frac{6}{10}$

C $\frac{4}{6}$

D $\frac{6}{4}$

☐ Kamessha's mother bought her 10 new T-shirts for school. Three of the 10, or $\frac{3}{10}$, of the shirts have polka dots. Which is the correct way to write that as a decimal?

A 0.3

B 10.3

C 1.03

D 0.03

☐ Russell spent $\frac{65}{100}$ of a dollar for a candy bar. Which tells how much he spent? Mark your answer.

A $65.00

B $0.65

C $6.50

D $0.065

Reporting Category 1 – 4.2 (G) Number and Operations

☐ **Mrs. Baker bought her children new clothes for school. Two of the items,**

or $\frac{2}{10}$, **are sweaters. Which is the correct way to write that amount as a decimal?**

Mark your answer.

A   0.02

B   2.10

C   0.2

D   2.0

Reporting Category 1 – 4.2 (G) Number and Operations

☐ **McKenna and Paul participated in a race. What is the correct way to write the distance Paul ran as a decimal? Mark your answer.**

A   150.00 miles

B   1.12 miles

C   0.50 mile

D   1.50 miles

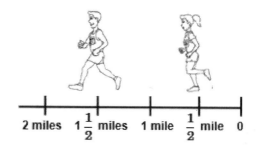

2 miles $1\frac{1}{2}$ miles   1 mile $\frac{1}{2}$ mile   0

Reporting Category 1 – 4.2 (G) Number and Operations

☐ **Jose gained 1.75 pounds last year. What is another way to write the number of pounds he gained? Mark your answer.**

A $1\frac{75}{10}$

B $1\frac{7}{5}$

C $1\frac{75}{100}$

D $\frac{1}{75}$

Reporting Category 1 – 4.2 (G) Number and Operations

☐ **Mr. Mason conducted a survey to find how people spent their time on the weekend. The survey showed 0.3 liked to read a book, 0.1 enjoyed working in their yard, and 0.6 liked to watch television. Which fraction shows how many people spent their time watching television? Mark your answer.**

A $\dfrac{10}{6}$ C $\dfrac{6}{10}$

B $\dfrac{60}{10}$ D $\dfrac{6}{100}$

Reporting Category 1 – 4.2 (G) Number and Operations

☐ **Mr. Taylor is putting tile in his kitchen. The job is 0.40 completed. Which fraction shows how much of the kitchen has completed? Mark your answer.**

A $\dfrac{60}{100}$

B $\dfrac{20}{100}$

C $\dfrac{40}{100}$

D $\dfrac{100}{60}$

Reporting Category 1 – 4.2 (G) Number and Operations

☐ **Which decimal represents $5\frac{3}{10}$? Mark your answer.**

A   5.310

B   5.3

C   0.5310

D   5.03

Reporting Category 1 – 4.2 (G) Number and Operations

☐ **Miss Alexander is an art teacher. She has used 0.8 of a tube of red paint, 0.5 of a tube of yellow paint, and 0.2 of a can of turpentine. Which fraction shows how much yellow paint she has used? Mark your answer.**

A $\dfrac{15}{10}$ C $\dfrac{5}{10}$

B $\dfrac{5}{100}$ D $\dfrac{10}{5}$

Reporting Category 1 – 4.2 (G) Number and Operations

☐ **Miss Milton picked 2.37 pounds of strawberries and 3.35 pounds of squash. What is another way to write the number of pounds of strawberries she picked? Mark your answer.**

A $2\dfrac{3}{7}$

B $2\dfrac{37}{100}$

C $3\dfrac{35}{100}$

D $3\dfrac{3}{5}$

Reporting Category 1 – 4.2 (G) Number and Operations

☐ **Jessie saved $\dfrac{25}{100}$ of a dollar last week and $\dfrac{79}{100}$ of a dollar today. Which tells the total amount of money he has saved? Mark your answer.**

A $0.54

B $0.94

C $10.40

D $1.04

Reporting Category 1 – 4.2 (H) Number and Operations

Which point best represents 16.3 on the number line below? Mark your answer.

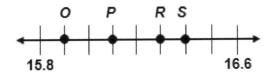

A   Point *S*   C   Point *O*

B   Point *R*   D   Point *P*

Reporting Category 1 – 4.2 (H) Number and Operations

Which number does point *X* best represent on the number line below? Mark your answer.

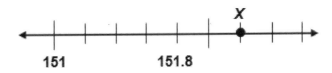

A   151   C   152.2

B   151.9   D   153

Reporting Category 1 – 4.2 (H) Number and Operations

Which number does point *Z* best represent on the number line below? Mark your answer.

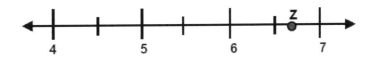

A   6.5

B   6.7

C   6.2

D   6.9

Reporting Category 1 – 4.2 (H) Number and Operations

☐ **Which number does point *T* best represent on the number line below? Mark your answer.**

A   3.4   C   3.5

B   3.8   D   3.6

Reporting Category 1 – 4.2 (H) Number and Operations

☐ **Point *M* best represents what number on the number line below? Mark your answer.**

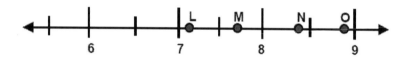

A   7.2   C   7.7

B   7.1   D   8.2

Reporting Category 1 – 4.2 (H) Number and Operations

☐ **Jeffrey walked 1.8 miles in a walk-a-thon. Which number line shows how far he walked? Mark your answer.**

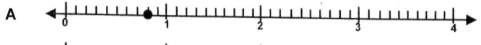

Reporting Category 1 – 4.2 (H) Number and Operations

☐ **Which point best represents 24.6 on the number line below? Mark your answer.**

A	Point *P*		C	Point *N*
B	Point *L*		D	Point *M*

Reporting Category 1 – 4.2 (H) Number and Operations

☐ **What number on the number line does point *L* best represent? Mark your answer.**

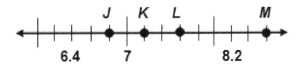

A	7.4		C	7.6
B	7.2		D	7.5

Reporting Category 1 – 4.2 (H) Number and Operations

☐ **An inchworm is racing along a number line. Which number tells how far the inchworm has gone? Mark your answer.**

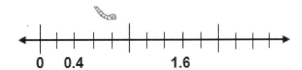

A   0.6

B   0.8

C   1.0

D   1.2

Reporting Category 1 – 4.2 (H) Number and Operations

☐ **What number on the number line does point *Y* best represent? Mark your answer.**

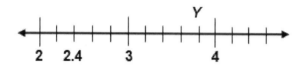

A	3.4	C	3.8
B	0.8	D	.3.0

Reporting Category 1 – 4.2 (H) Number and Operations

☐ **Which point best represents 25.7 on the number line? Mark your answer.**

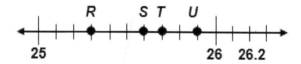

A	Point *U*	C	Point *R*
B	Point *T*	D	Point *S*

Reporting Category 1 – 4.2 (H) Number and Operations

☐ **Point *B* best represents what number on the number line below? Mark your answer.**

A 11.1

B 11.6

C 11.4

D 11.8

Reporting Category 1 – 4.3 (A) Number and Operations

☐ How many fractions of $\frac{1}{16}$ are there in the fraction $\frac{23}{16}$? Mark your answer.

A   7

B   16

C   21

D   23

Reporting Category 1 – 4.3 (A) Number and Operations

☐ Which is the correct way of writing the fraction $\frac{7}{17}$? Mark your answer.

A $\frac{1}{17} + \frac{1}{17} + \frac{1}{17} + \frac{1}{17} + \frac{1}{17} + \frac{1}{17}$

B $\frac{1}{17} + \frac{1}{17} + \frac{1}{17} + \frac{1}{17} + \frac{1}{17} + \frac{1}{17} + \frac{1}{17}$

C $\frac{2}{17} + \frac{2}{17} + \frac{2}{17} + \frac{2}{17} + \frac{2}{17} + \frac{2}{17}$

D $\frac{2}{17} + \frac{2}{17} + \frac{2}{17} + \frac{2}{17} + \frac{2}{17} + \frac{2}{17} + \frac{1}{17}$

Reporting Category 1 – 4.3 (A) Number and Operations

☐ One centimeter is equal to $\frac{1}{100}$ meter. How many centimeters are in $\frac{76}{100}$ meter? Mark your answer.

A   67

B   76

C   34

D   24

Reporting Category 1 – 4.3 (A) Number and Operations

☐ **Which equation below is true? Mark your answer.**

A $\frac{5}{6} = \frac{1}{5} + \frac{1}{5} + \frac{1}{5} + \frac{1}{5} + \frac{1}{5} + \frac{1}{5}$

B $\frac{5}{6} = \frac{1}{5} + \frac{1}{5} + \frac{1}{5} + \frac{1}{5} + \frac{1}{5}$

C $\frac{7}{11} = \frac{1}{11} + \frac{1}{11} + \frac{1}{11} + \frac{1}{11} + \frac{1}{11} + \frac{1}{11} + \frac{1}{11}$

D $\frac{7}{11} = \frac{1}{7} + \frac{1}{7} + \frac{1}{7} + \frac{1}{7} + \frac{1}{7} + \frac{1}{7} + \frac{1}{7}$

Reporting Category 1 – 4.3 (H) Number and Operations

☐ **To find $\frac{39}{29} - \frac{19}{29}$, we can do which of the following operations? Mark your answer.**

A   **Find 20 times $\frac{1}{29}$.**

B   **Find 58 times $\frac{1}{29}$.**

C   **Find 10 times $\frac{1}{29}$.**

D   **Find 20 times $\frac{1}{19}$.**

Reporting Category 1 – 4.3 (A) Number and Operations

☐ **Which statement below is true? Mark your answer.**

A $\frac{6}{5}$ is made up of six of $\frac{5}{7}$, and $\frac{5}{6}$ is made up of five of $\frac{6}{5}$.

B $\frac{7}{5}$ is made up of five of $\frac{1}{7}$, and $\frac{5}{6}$ is made up of five of $\frac{1}{7}$.

C $\frac{6}{5}$ is made up of six of $\frac{1}{5}$, and $\frac{5}{6}$ is made up of five of $\frac{1}{6}$.

D $\frac{9}{5}$ is made up of 9 of $\frac{1}{9}$, and $\frac{5}{8}$ is made up of five of $\frac{1}{8}$.

Reporting Category 1 – 4.3 (A) Number and Operations

A meatball made up of beef and pork. Their weights are:

Beef: $(\frac{1}{29} + \frac{1}{29} + \frac{1}{29} + \frac{1}{29})$ pounds

Pork: $(\frac{1}{29} + \frac{1}{29} + \frac{1}{29} + \frac{1}{29} + \frac{1}{29} + \frac{1}{29})$ pounds.

Which is the total weight of the meat ball? Mark your answer.

A $\frac{9}{29}$ C $\frac{13}{29}$

B $\frac{10}{29}$ D $\frac{15}{29}$

Reporting Category 1 – 4.3 (A) Number and Operations

Each cup of sugar weighs $\frac{1}{29}$ pounds. Which statement helps you to find out how many cups are in $\frac{9}{29}$ pounds sugar? Mark your answer.

A $\frac{9}{29} + \frac{9}{29} + \frac{9}{29} + \frac{9}{29} + \frac{9}{29} + \frac{9}{29} + \frac{9}{29} + \frac{9}{29} + \frac{9}{29}$

B $\frac{9}{29} + \frac{9}{29} + \frac{9}{29} + \frac{9}{29} + \frac{9}{29} + \frac{9}{29} + \frac{9}{29} + \frac{9}{29}$

C $\frac{1}{29} + \frac{1}{29} + \frac{1}{29} + \frac{1}{29} + \frac{1}{29} + \frac{1}{29} + \frac{1}{29} + \frac{1}{29} + \frac{1}{29}$

D $\frac{1}{29} + \frac{1}{29} + \frac{1}{29} + \frac{1}{29} + \frac{1}{29} + \frac{1}{29} + \frac{1}{29} + \frac{1}{29}$

Reporting Category 1 – 4.3 (A) Number and Operations

Which fractions are missing from $\frac{7}{5} = \frac{1}{5} + \frac{1}{5} + \frac{1}{5} + \frac{1}{5} + \boxed{} + \boxed{} + \frac{1}{5}$? Mark your answer.

A $\frac{1}{7}$ and $\frac{1}{7}$ C $\frac{1}{5}$ and $\frac{1}{5}$

B $\frac{5}{7}$ and $\frac{5}{7}$ D $\frac{7}{1}$ and $\frac{7}{1}$

Reporting Category 1 – 4.3 (A) Number and Operations

☐ The shaded cells in the figure below represent $\frac{23}{16}$.

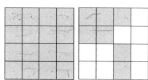

What fraction represents each cell? Mark your answer.

A $\frac{2}{16}$ C $\frac{3}{18}$

B $\frac{1}{16}$ D $\frac{1}{18}$

Reporting Category 1 – 4.3 (A) Number and Operations

☐ Each slice of a pizza is $\frac{1}{6}$ of the pizza. If $\frac{5}{6}$ of the pizza is eaten, how many slices are eaten? Mark your answer.

A   7

B   6

C   5

D   4

Reporting Category 1 – 4.3 (A) Number and Operations

☐ If each square is equal to $\frac{1}{5}$, which of the answers below are true? Mark your answer.

A $= \frac{9}{5}$ C $= \frac{8}{5}$

B $= \frac{9}{5}$ D $= \frac{6}{5}$

Name _____

DIAGNOSTIC

Reporting Category 1 – 4.3 (B) Number and Operations

[ ] **Which of the models shows the fraction $\frac{1}{2}$? Mark your answer.**

A 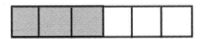   C

B 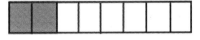   D

Reporting Category 1 – 4.3 (B) Number and Operations

[ ] **Which model does *not* show the fraction $\frac{1}{4}$? Mark your answer.**

A    C

B    D

Reporting Category 1 – 4.3 (B) Number and Operations

[ ] **Which of the models shows the fraction $\frac{2}{3}$? Mark your answer.**

A 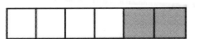   C

B   D

© Teachers' Treasures Publishing

Page 51

Reporting Category 1 – 4.3 (B) Number and Operations

☐ Which of the models shows the fraction $\frac{3}{5}$? Mark your answer.

A 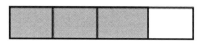   C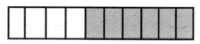

B    D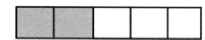

Reporting Category 1 – 4.3 (B) Number and Operations

☐ Which model does *not* show the fraction $\frac{1}{6}$? Mark your answer.

A 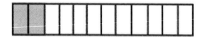   C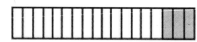

B 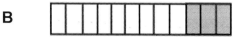   D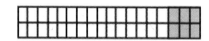

Reporting Category 1 – 4.3 (B) Number and Operations

☐ Which model does *not* show the fraction $\frac{3}{4}$? Mark your answer.

A    C

B    D

Name _____

PRACTICE

Reporting Category 1 – 4.3 (B) Number and Operations

☐ **Which of the models shows the fraction $\frac{3}{9}$? Mark your answer.**

A 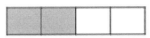   C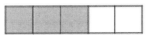

B    D

Reporting Category 1 – 4.3 (B) Number and Operations

☐ **Which model does *not* show the fraction $\frac{12}{16}$? Mark your answer.**

A    C

B    D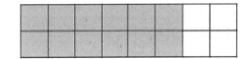

Reporting Category 1 – 4.3 (B) Number and Operations

☐ **Which model shows the fraction $\frac{1}{8}$? Mark your answer.**

A   C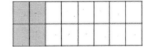

B   D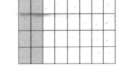

© Teachers' Treasures Publishing

Page 53

Reporting Category 1 – 4.3 (B) Number and Operations

Which of the models shows the fraction $\frac{1}{4}$? Mark your answer.

A

C

B

D

Reporting Category 1 – 4.3 (B) Number and Operations

Which of the models shows $\frac{9}{12}$? Mark your answer.

A

C

B

D

Reporting Category 1 – 4.3 (B) Number and Operations

Which model shows the fraction $\frac{15}{21}$? Mark your answer.

A

C

B

D

Reporting Category 1 – 4.3 (C) Number and Operations

☐ **Which fraction represents the shaded part of the model below? Mark your answer.**

A $\dfrac{4}{5}$ C $\dfrac{4}{4}$

B $\dfrac{1}{5}$ D $\dfrac{1}{4}$

Reporting Category 1 – 4.3 (C) Number and Operations

☐ **The model is shaded to represent a fraction.**

Which model below shows an equivalent fraction? Mark your answer.

A   C

B   D

Reporting Category 1 – 4.3 (C) Number and Operations

☐ **Which model is shaded to show a fraction equivalent to $\dfrac{1}{4}$? Mark your answer.**

A   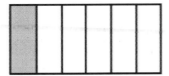   C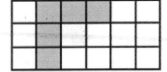

B      D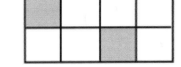

Reporting Category 1 – 4.3 (C) Number and Operations

Which pair of figures shows equivalent fractions? Mark your answer.

A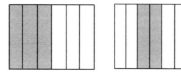

B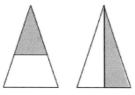

C

D

Reporting Category 1 – 4.3 (C) Number and Operations

Which statement is true? Mark your answer.

A

B

C

D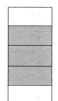

Reporting Category 1 – 4.3 (C) Number and Operations

Which model is shaded to show a fraction equivalent to 1/3? Mark your answer.

A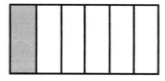

B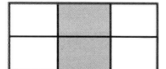

C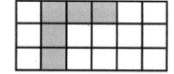

D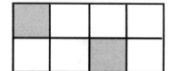

Reporting Category 1 – 4.3 (C) Number and Operations

Which model is shaded to show a fraction equivalent to $\frac{2}{3}$? Mark your answer.

A 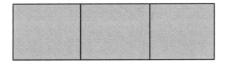   C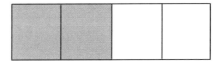

B    D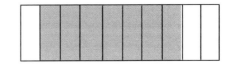

Reporting Category 1 – 4.3 (C) Number and Operations

Which pair of figures shows equivalent fractions? Mark your answer.

A 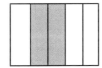   C

B 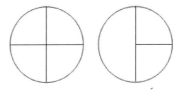   D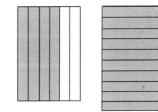

Reporting Category 1 – 4.3 (C) Number and Operations

The model is shaded to represent a fraction.

Which model below shows an equivalent fraction? Mark your answer.

A   C

B   D

Reporting Category 1 – 4.3 (C) Number and Operations

☐ **Which statement is NOT true? Mark your answer.**

A =   C >

B =   D =

Reporting Category 1 – 4.3 (C) Number and Operations

☐ **Which pair of figures shows equivalent fractions? Mark your answer.**

A   C

B   D

Reporting Category 1 – 4.3 (C) Number and Operations

☐ **Which fraction represents the unshaded part of the model below? Mark your answer.**

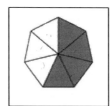

A $\frac{4}{7}$ C $\frac{3}{7}$

B $\frac{3}{4}$ D $\frac{4}{3}$

Reporting Category 1 – 4.3 (D) Number and Operations

☐ Mr. Turner painted three rooms in his house. He painted the garage gray, the living room blue, and the kitchen yellow. He has $\frac{3}{4}$ gallon of yellow paint, $\frac{1}{2}$ gallon of blue paint, and $\frac{3}{8}$ gallon of gray paint left after he finished painting all of the rooms. If he places the containers of paint in order from the least to the greatest amount, which of the following would be correct? Mark your answer.

A   Gray, yellow, blue

B   Blue, yellow, gray

C   Yellow, blue, gray

D   Gray, blue, yellow

Reporting Category 1 – 4.3 (D) Number and Operations

☐ Which statement can be used to show a comparison of $\frac{3}{12}$ and $\frac{2}{8}$? Mark your answer.

A $\frac{3}{12}$ is greater than $\frac{2}{8}$ C $\frac{2}{8}$ is equal to $\frac{3}{12}$

B $\frac{2}{8}$ is less than $\frac{3}{12}$ D $\frac{3}{12}$ is less than $\frac{2}{8}$

Reporting Category 1 – 4.3 (D) Number and Operations

☐ Wyatt is comparing fractions using models his teacher gave him. If he wants to prove that $\frac{2}{6}$ is less than $\frac{2}{3}$, which models should he use? Mark your answer.

    1   2   3   4

A   2 and 4   C   1 and 4

B   2 and 3   D   1 and 3

Reporting Category 1 – 4.3 (D) Number and Operations

☐ **Look at the shaded parts of the two shapes. Which statement shows this fraction model? Mark your answer.**

A $\frac{1}{3} > \frac{3}{9}$

B $\frac{1}{3} < \frac{3}{9}$

C $\frac{1}{3} = \frac{3}{9}$

D $\frac{1}{3} > \frac{4}{12}$

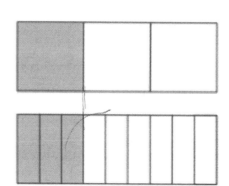

Reporting Category 1 – 4.3 (D) Number and Operations

☐ **Some of the girls in Miss Monroe and Ms. Baker's classes have cats and dogs for pets. Which statement is a correct comparison of the number of girls who have dogs as a pet? Mark your answer.**

A $\frac{2}{5} = \frac{7}{12}$

B $\frac{7}{12} > \frac{2}{5}$

C $\frac{7}{12} < \frac{2}{5}$

D $\frac{4}{10} < \frac{2}{5}$

Ms. Baker's Class

Miss Monroe's Class

Reporting Category 1 – 4.3 (D) Number and Operations

☐ **The shapes are shaded to show that _____. Mark your answer.**

A $\frac{1}{4} < \frac{1}{5}$ C $\frac{3}{4} > \frac{7}{8}$

B $\frac{7}{8} > \frac{3}{4}$ D $\frac{1}{8} > \frac{1}{4}$

Name _____

Reporting Category 1 – 4.3 (D) Number and Operations

☐ **Alex's family ordered two pizzas. The models show the amount of pizza left after the family finished eating dinner. Which of the following compares the amount of slices left in each pizza? Mark your answer.**

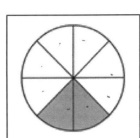 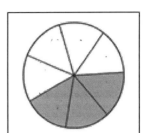

A $\frac{1}{4} < \frac{3}{7}$

B $\frac{2}{6} > \frac{3}{4}$

C $\frac{2}{8} < \frac{3}{8}$

D $\frac{3}{7} < \frac{2}{8}$

Reporting Category 1 – 4.3 (D) Number and Operations

☐ **Which shows the figures in order from least to greatest? Mark your answer.**

A $\frac{5}{8}, \frac{3}{8}, \frac{3}{4}$ C $\frac{3}{4}, \frac{3}{8}, \frac{5}{8}$

B $\frac{3}{8}, \frac{3}{4}, \frac{5}{8}$ D $\frac{3}{8}, \frac{5}{8}, \frac{3}{4}$

Reporting Category 1 – 4.3 (D) Number and Operations

☐ **Which statement represents the shaded models? Mark your answer.**

A $\frac{2}{5} = \frac{7}{10} = \frac{2}{6}$ C $\frac{2}{5} > \frac{7}{10} > \frac{2}{6}$

B $\frac{7}{10} > \frac{2}{5} > \frac{2}{6}$ D $\frac{2}{3} < \frac{2}{4} < \frac{3}{7}$

Reporting Category 1 – 4.3 (D) Number and Operations

☐ Alicia's friends believe $\frac{3}{4}$ is greater than $\frac{2}{3}$. Which two models can be used to prove Alicia's friends are correct? Mark your answer.

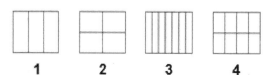

 1 2 3 4

A   1 and 3   C   1 and 2

B   3 and 4   D   2 and 3

Reporting Category 1 – 4.3 (D) Number and Operations

☐ Which statement can be used to show a comparison of $\frac{6}{8}$ and $\frac{5}{15}$? Mark your answer.

A $\frac{5}{15}$ is greater than $\frac{6}{8}$ C $\frac{5}{15}$ is equal to $\frac{6}{8}$

B $\frac{6}{8}$ is less than $\frac{5}{15}$ D $\frac{6}{8}$ is greater than $\frac{5}{15}$

Reporting Category 1 – 4.3 (D) Number and Operations

☐ Mrs. Sanchez baked a chocolate, pecan, and coconut pie for Thanksgiving. Her guests ate $\frac{4}{10}$ of the chocolate pie, $\frac{3}{8}$ of the coconut pie, and $\frac{3}{4}$ of the pecan pie. If Mrs. Sanchez places the pies in order from least to greatest amount of pie eaten, which of the following represents the order of the pies? Mark your answer.

A   Pecan, coconut, chocolate

B   Pecan, chocolate, coconut

C   Chocolate, coconut, pecan

D   Coconut, chocolate, pecan

Name _____

Reporting Category 1 – 4.3 (H) Number and Operations

Which point on the number line best represents $22\frac{3}{4}$? Mark your answer.

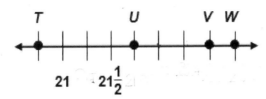

A	Point *V*	C	Point *T*
B	Point *U*	D	Point *W*

Reporting Category 1 – 4.3 (H) Number and Operations

What number on the number line does point *S* best represent? Mark your answer.

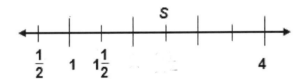

A	2	C	$3\frac{1}{2}$
B	3	D	$2\frac{1}{2}$

Reporting Category 1 – 4.3 (H) Number and Operations

Which object on the number line is at a position greater than $\frac{6}{8}$? Mark your answer.

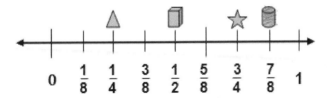

A	Triangle	C	Star
B	Cylinder	D	Cube

Reporting Category 1 – 4.3 (H) Number and Operations

☐ Which object on the number line is at a position less than $2\frac{4}{6}$? Mark your answer.

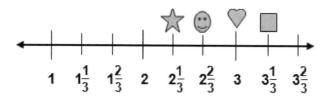

A   Face   C   Heart

B   Star   D   Square

Reporting Category 1 – 4.3 (H) Number and Operations

☐ What number on the number line does point X best represent? Mark your answer.

A   5   C $5\frac{1}{2}$

B   4   D $6\frac{1}{2}$

Reporting Category 1 – 4.3 (H) Number and Operations

☐ Which point on the number line best represents $8\frac{6}{8}$? Mark your answer.

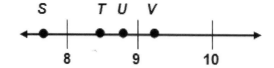

A   Point V   C   Point U

B   Point S   D   Point T

Reporting Category 1 – 4.3 (H) Number and Operations

☐ **Point T best represents which number? Mark your answer.**

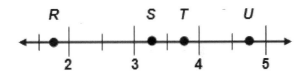

A $3\frac{3}{4}$ C $3\frac{1}{4}$

B $3\frac{1}{2}$ D $4\frac{3}{4}$

Reporting Category 1 – 4.3 (H) Number and Operations

☐ **Which point on the number line best represents $10\frac{3}{4}$? Mark your answer.**

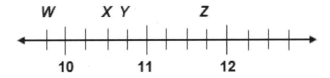

A Point Z   C Point W

B Point X   D Point Y

Reporting Category 1 – 4.3 (H) Number and Operations

☐ **Which object on the number line is at a position less than $1\frac{1}{3}$? Mark your answer.**

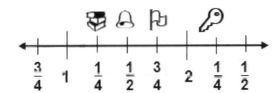

A Key   C Books

B Bell   D Flag

Reporting Category 1 – 4.3 (H) Number and Operations

☐ Which point on the number line best represents $23\frac{2}{3}$? Mark your answer.

A	Point D	C	Point A
B	Point B	D	Point C

Reporting Category 1 – 4.3 (H) Number and Operations

☐ Which object on the number line is at a position less than $\frac{4}{8}$ and greater than $\frac{1}{8}$? Mark your answer.

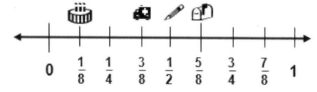

A	Pencil	C	Birthday cake
B	Ambulance	D	Mailbox

Reporting Category 1 – 4.3 (H) Number and Operations

☐ What number on the number line does point A best represent? Mark your answer.

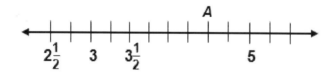

A	$4\frac{1}{4}$	C	4
B	$3\frac{1}{4}$	D	$4\frac{1}{2}$

Name _____

Reporting Category 2 – 4.3 (E) Number and Operations

☐ Jose had 8 nickels left when he bought a magazine. He spent 3 of the nickels for a pencil and 4 nickels for a cookie. What fraction represents the number of nickels he had left? Mark your answer.

A $\frac{7}{8}$ C $\frac{5}{8}$

B $\frac{1}{8}$ D $\frac{4}{8}$

Reporting Category 2 – 4.3 (E) Number and Operations

☐ Wendy bought a box of candy for her mother. If her mother has eaten $\frac{5}{8}$ of the candy, what fraction of candy is left? Mark your answer.

A $\frac{3}{8}$ C $\frac{2}{8}$

B $\frac{9}{8}$ D $\frac{4}{8}$

Reporting Category 2 – 4.3 (E) Number and Operations

☐ Wyatt's grandfather bought 10 sacks of grass seed to put on his lawn. He spread $\frac{3}{10}$ of the sacks on Friday and $\frac{4}{10}$ of the sacks of grass seed on Saturday. If he spreads the remaining sacks next week, what fraction represents the remaining sacks? Mark your answer.

A $\frac{7}{10}$ C $\frac{3}{10}$

B $\frac{6}{10}$ D $\frac{7}{20}$

Reporting Category 2 – 4.3 (E) Number and Operations

William has completed $\frac{3}{8}$ of his homework, and Brent has completed $\frac{7}{8}$ of his homework. What fraction of his homework does Brent still need to complete? Mark your answer.

A $\frac{5}{8}$ C $\frac{10}{16}$

B $\frac{10}{8}$ D $\frac{1}{8}$

Reporting Category 2 – 4.3 (E) Number and Operations

The table below shows the number of different kinds of magazines a store sold. In all, what fraction of the number of magazines sold were sports and cooking magazines? Mark your answer.

A $\frac{18}{62}$

B $\frac{18}{31}$

C $\frac{11}{31}$

D $\frac{13}{18}$

Kind of Magazine	Number Sold
Decorating	9
Cooking	7
Financial	4
Sports	11

Reporting Category 2 – 4.3 (E) Number and Operations

A pepperoni pizza and a sausage pizza were each divided into 8 equal slices. The shaded parts of the models below show the part of each pizza that was eaten at Kathryn's birthday party. Which of the following number sentences can be used to find how much more sausage pizza was eaten than pepperoni pizza? Mark your answer.

A $\frac{6}{8} + \frac{5}{8} = \frac{11}{8}$

B $\frac{3}{8} - \frac{2}{8} = \frac{1}{8}$

C $\frac{6}{8} - \frac{5}{8} = \frac{1}{8}$

D $\frac{3}{5} - \frac{2}{6} = \frac{1}{11}$

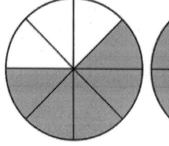
Pepperoni Pizza

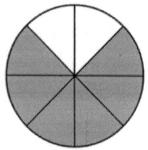
Sausage Pizza

Reporting Category 2 – 4.3 (E) Number and Operations

☐ Jason saved his allowance to buy a video game. When he priced the game, it cost $15. He has only saved $\frac{3}{5}$ of the cost of the game. What fraction below represents the amount he needs to save to buy the video game? Mark your answer.

A $\frac{3}{5}$

C $\frac{5}{3}$

B $\frac{45}{75}$

D $\frac{2}{5}$

Reporting Category 2 – 4.3 (E) Number and Operations

☐ Ms. Monroe bought 22 shrubs at a nursery. She bought 6 rose bushes, 3 azalea plants, and 4 holly plants. What fraction below represents the number of plants that are not rose and holly bushes? Mark your answer.

A $\frac{9}{22}$

C $\frac{13}{22}$

B $\frac{10}{22}$

D $\frac{12}{22}$

Reporting Category 2 – 4.3 (E) Number and Operations

☐ Mark sorted and counted his markers. The table below shows the colors of markers he has and the number of each marker. In all, what fraction below is the number of blue and green markers he has? Mark your answer.

A $\frac{7}{20}$

B $\frac{9}{20}$

C $\frac{13}{20}$

D $\frac{10}{20}$

Color of Marker	Number of Markers
Yellow	4
Green	7
Red	3
Blue	6

Name _____

Reporting Category 2 – 4.3 (E) Number and Operations

A school cafeteria made a dozen tuna fish, pimento, and chicken salad sandwiches. The students ate $\frac{3}{12}$ of the chicken salad sandwiches and $\frac{2}{12}$ of the tuna fish sandwiches. What fraction of the pimento sandwiches were eaten? Mark your answer.

A $\quad \frac{5}{12}$

C $\quad \frac{7}{12}$

B $\quad \frac{9}{12}$

D $\quad \frac{19}{12}$

Reporting Category 2 – 4.3 (E) Number and Operations

Leah divided two boxes into 5 equal parts. The shaded parts of the models below show the part of each box where Leah placed a necklace. Which of the following number sentences can be used to find how many more necklaces were placed in Box B than in Box A? Mark your answer.

A $\quad \frac{5}{5} - \frac{2}{5} = \frac{3}{5}$

B $\quad \frac{4}{5} - \frac{2}{5} = \frac{2}{5}$

C $\quad \frac{3}{5} - \frac{1}{5} = \frac{2}{5}$

D $\quad \frac{4}{5} + \frac{2}{5} = \frac{6}{5}$

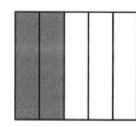
Box A

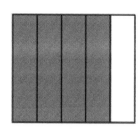
Box B

Reporting Category 2 – 4.3 (E) Number and Operations

Maria ate $\frac{5}{9}$ of a pizza and her brother ate $\frac{2}{9}$ of the same pizza. What fraction of the entire pizza did they eat? Mark your answer.

A $\quad \frac{2}{9}$

C $\quad \frac{3}{9}$

B $\quad \frac{7}{9}$

D $\quad \frac{7}{18}$

Reporting Category 2 – 4.3 (E) Number and Operations

☐ Gabrielle and her friends bought a candy bar to share. Gabrielle ate $\frac{1}{6}$ of the candy bar, Sarah ate $\frac{2}{6}$ of the candy bar, and Jared ate $\frac{1}{3}$ of it. How much of the candy bar was left? Mark your answer.

A $\frac{2}{6}$ C $\frac{4}{6}$

B $\frac{5}{6}$ D $\frac{1}{6}$

Reporting Category 2 – 4.3 (E) Number and Operations

☐ Matthew and Ben shared a cheese sandwich. Matthew ate $\frac{3}{8}$ of the sandwich, and Ben ate $\frac{1}{8}$ of the sandwich. What fraction of the sandwich did the boys eat? Mark your answer.

A $\frac{1}{4}$ C $\frac{5}{8}$

B $\frac{1}{2}$ D $\frac{4}{16}$

Reporting Category 2 – 4.3 (E) Number and Operations

☐ The shaded parts of the shapes below represent the amount of coins Katie has put in a coin album. Which of the following number sentences can be used to find how many more coins are on Page A than on Page B? Mark your answer.

A $\frac{4}{10} + \frac{2}{10} = \frac{6}{10}$

B $\frac{4}{10} - \frac{2}{10} = \frac{2}{10}$

C $\frac{6}{10} + \frac{8}{10} = \frac{14}{10}$

D $\frac{8}{10} - \frac{2}{10} = \frac{6}{10}$

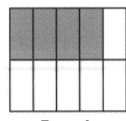
Page A

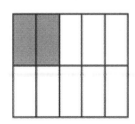
Page B

Reporting Category 2 – 4.3 (E) Number and Operations

☐ **Mrs. Sanders stored Christmas ornaments in boxes after Christmas. She put $\frac{2}{6}$ of the ornaments in a paper box and $\frac{3}{6}$ of the ornaments in a plastic container. If she packed the remaining ornaments in a wooden box, what fraction of the ornaments were placed in the wooden box? Mark your answer.**

A $\frac{5}{6}$ C $\frac{1}{6}$

B $\frac{5}{12}$ D $\frac{4}{6}$

Reporting Category 2 – 4.3 (E) Number and Operations

☐ **Mr. Long bought 11 books at an estate sale. He bought 2 books about cowboys and 4 atlases. He also found 3 nonfiction books about his favorite actor. What fraction of the books are not about his favorite actor and cowboys? Mark your answer.**

A $\frac{6}{11}$ C $\frac{9}{11}$

B $\frac{5}{11}$ D $\frac{3}{11}$

Reporting Category 2 – 4.3 (E) Number and Operations

☐ **The table below shows the number of books read by 4 students during the summer holidays. In all, what fraction below represents the number of books read by Lily and Valerie? Mark your answer.**

A $\frac{12}{27}$

B $\frac{15}{27}$

C $\frac{11}{27}$

D $\frac{16}{27}$

Student	Number of Books
Valerie	9
Bailey	6
Lily	7
Lucas	5

Reporting Category 2 – 4.3 (E) Number and Operations

☐ **Griffin helped the school librarian for two weeks. The first week he worked $6\frac{1}{2}$ hours and $3\frac{1}{4}$ hours the next week. Which of the number sentences can be used to find how much longer he worked the first week than the second week? Mark your answer.**

A $\quad 6\frac{1}{2} - 3\frac{1}{4} = 3\frac{1}{6}$

C $\quad 6\frac{2}{4} - 3\frac{1}{4} = 3\frac{1}{4}$

B $\quad 6\frac{2}{4} + 3\frac{1}{4} = 3\frac{3}{4}$

D $\quad 6\frac{1}{2} + 3\frac{1}{4} = 9\frac{2}{6}$

Reporting Category 2 – 4.3 (E) Number and Operations

☐ **The table below shows the number of balloons a store used each day to celebrate its grand opening. In all, what fraction of the number of balloons is equivalent to $\frac{2}{3}$? Mark your answer.**

A $\quad \frac{9}{27}$

B $\quad \frac{18}{27}$

C $\quad \frac{17}{27}$

D $\quad \frac{10}{27}$

Weekday	Number of Balloons
Friday	6
Saturday	12
Sunday	5
Monday	4

Reporting Category 2 – 4.3 (E) Number and Operations

☐ **Ms. Conners read $\frac{2}{7}$ of a book on Saturday. On Monday, she read $\frac{3}{7}$ of the book. What fraction represents the amount she had not read? Mark your answer.**

A $\quad \frac{5}{7}$

C $\quad \frac{1}{7}$

B $\quad \frac{3}{7}$

D $\quad \frac{2}{7}$

Reporting Category 2 – 4.3 (E) Number and Operations

☐ A school cafeteria ordered seven bags of sugar. They used $\frac{1}{2}$ of the total number of bags the first week of school. The next week they used $2\frac{1}{4}$ bags of the original order. How much sugar does the cafeteria have left? Mark your answer.

A $2\frac{1}{4}$ bags   C $1\frac{3}{4}$ bags

B $1\frac{1}{4}$ bags   D $3\frac{3}{4}$ bags

Reporting Category 2 – 4.3 (E) Number and Operations

☐ Macey's mother made fruit punch for a school party. The graph shows the amount of each kind of juice she used to make the punch. How much of the punch did not contain grape and apple juice? Mark your answer.

A $\frac{1}{2}$

B $\frac{5}{8}$

C $\frac{3}{8}$

D $\frac{4}{8}$

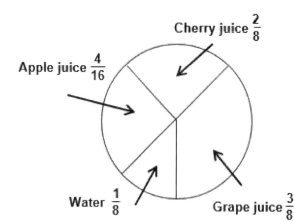

Reporting Category 2 – 4.3 (E) Number and Operations

☐ Alex saves old coins. He has 2 quarters dated 1941, 1 dime date 1908, and 4 nickels dated 1937. The remaining 5 coins are dated after 1970. What fraction of the coins are dated after 1940? Mark your answer.

A $\frac{7}{12}$ C $\frac{5}{7}$

B $\frac{5}{12}$ D $\frac{10}{12}$

Reporting Category 2 – 4.3 (F) Number and Operations

☐ Theodore Roosevelt Elementary 3ʳᵈ and 4ᵗʰ grade students are creating a chalk picture in front of the school. The third grade students colored ¼ of the picture and the fourth grade students colored ¼ of the picture. How much did the third and fourth grade student color on the picture all together? Mark your answer.

A $\frac{1}{4}$

C $\frac{3}{4}$

B $\frac{1}{2}$

D $\frac{2}{8}$

Reporting Category 2 – 4.3 (F) Number and Operations

☐ Subtract the fractions and simplify your answers. Be sure to show your work.

$$\frac{8}{16} - \frac{6}{16} = \square$$

A $\frac{1}{16}$

C $\frac{7}{8}$

B $\frac{1}{8}$

D $\frac{1}{4}$

Reporting Category 2 – 4.3 (F) Number and Operations

☐ Add the fractions and simplify your answers. Be sure to show your work.

$$\frac{9}{27} + \frac{6}{27} = \square$$

A $\frac{5}{9}$

C $\frac{1}{3}$

B $\frac{1}{9}$

D $\frac{2}{3}$

Name _____

Reporting Category 2 – 4.3 (F) Number and Operations

☐ Isaac bought $\frac{4}{7}$ kg of apples and $\frac{3}{7}$ kg of mangos. How much more did the apples weigh than the mangos? Mark your answer.

A $\frac{7}{7}$ C $\frac{1}{7}$

B $\frac{7}{14}$ D 1

Reporting Category 2 – 4.3 (F) Number and Operations

☐ **Add the fractions and simplify your answers. Mark your answer.**

$$\frac{10}{15} + \frac{7}{15} = \boxed{}$$

A $\frac{7}{15}$ C $\frac{1}{5}$

B $\frac{1}{10}$ D $\frac{17}{15}$

Reporting Category 2 – 4.3 (F) Number and Operations

☐ **Subtract the fractions and simplify your answers. Mark your answer.**

$$\frac{19}{29} - \frac{11}{29} = \boxed{}$$

A $\frac{8}{29}$ C $\frac{30}{29}$

B $\frac{29}{29}$ D $\frac{7}{29}$

Name _____

Reporting Category 2 – 4.3 (F) Number and Operations

☐ **Jarrell and his brother Makal are working on a jigsaw together. Jarrell has finished one quarter of the jigsaw, and Makal has finished two quarters of the jigsaw. How much of the jigsaw have they finished all together? Mark your answer.**

A $\dfrac{1}{4}$ 　　　　　　　　C $\dfrac{1}{2}$

B $\dfrac{3}{4}$ 　　　　　　　　D $\dfrac{2}{3}$

Reporting Category 2 – 4.3 (F) Number and Operations

☐ **Add the fractions and simplify your answers. Mark your answer.**

$$\dfrac{14}{57} + \dfrac{27}{57} = \square$$

A $\dfrac{14}{57}$ 　　　　　　　　C $\dfrac{42}{57}$

B $\dfrac{9}{19}$ 　　　　　　　　D $\dfrac{41}{57}$

Reporting Category 2 – 4.3 (F) Number and Operations

☐ **Gary and Beth's mother baked a cake. Gary eats one third of the cake and Beth eats one third of the cake. How much did Gary and Beth eat all together? Mark your answer.**

A $\dfrac{2}{3}$ 　　　　　　　　C $\dfrac{1}{3}$

B $\dfrac{1}{2}$ 　　　　　　　　D $\dfrac{1}{9}$

Reporting Category 2 – 4.3 (F) Number and Operations

☐ Macy and her friend ran around the track together. Macy ran 6/10's of the track. Her friend ran 9/10's of the track. How much further did Macy's friend run than Macy? Mark your answer.

A $\frac{1}{4}$

C $\frac{3}{10}$

B $\frac{3}{2}$

D $\frac{3}{4}$

Reporting Category 2 – 4.3 (F) Number and Operations

☐ Subtract the fractions and simplify your answers. Mark your answer.

$$\frac{7}{34} - \frac{3}{34} = \boxed{}$$

A $\frac{5}{32}$

C $\frac{5}{17}$

B $\frac{10}{17}$

D $\frac{2}{17}$

Reporting Category 2 – 4.3 (F) Number and Operations

☐ Happy Burger restaurant had $\frac{5}{9}$ ground beef yesterday, but today there is only $\frac{2}{9}$ ground beef left. How much ground beef was used today to make hamburgers? Mark your answer.

A $\frac{3}{9}$

C $\frac{7}{18}$

B $\frac{7}{9}$

D $\frac{1}{9}$

Name _____

Common Core Standard 4.NF.3 – Number & Operations – Fractions

☐ In the morning Carkye and her sister Candice eat breakfast burritos. Carkye ate $3\frac{4}{7}$ breakfast burritos. Her sister Candice ate $2\frac{3}{7}$ breakfast burritos. How many more breakfast burritos did Carkye eat than her sister Candice? Mark your answer.

A $1\frac{1}{7}$

C 1

B $\frac{17}{7}$

D $\frac{24}{7}$

Reporting Category 2 – 4.3 (F) Number and Operations

☐ Subtract the fractions and simplify your answers. Mark your answer.

$$\frac{24}{54} - \frac{15}{54} = \boxed{}$$

A $\frac{1}{9}$

C $\frac{39}{108}$

B $\frac{1}{6}$

D $\frac{39}{54}$

Reporting Category 2 – 4.3 (F) Number and Operations

☐ Henrietta is making mashed potatoes for her family. Her brothers eat 4/7 the mashed potatoes and her sisters eat 3/7 of the mashed potatoes. How much more mashed potatoes did her brothers eat than her sisters? Mark your answer.

A $\frac{1}{7}$

C 1

B $\frac{1}{2}$

D $\frac{2}{7}$

Reporting Category 2 – 4.3 (F) Number and Operations

☐ At Early Bird coffee shop, 3/8 of the customer's order only tea. 4/8 of the customer's order only coffee. What fraction of the customer's order only tea or coffee? Mark your answer.

A $\dfrac{1}{8}$ C $\dfrac{7}{16}$

B $\dfrac{1}{2}$ D $\dfrac{7}{8}$

Reporting Category 2 – 4.3 (F) Number and Operations

☐ Add the fractions and simplify your answers. Mark your answer.

$$\dfrac{17}{61} + \dfrac{33}{61} = \square$$

A $\dfrac{50}{61}$ C $\dfrac{25}{61}$

B $\dfrac{16}{61}$ D $\dfrac{40}{61}$

Reporting Category 2 – 4.3 (F) Number and Operations

☐ Seth went to the grocery store and bought 4/7 kg of sugar and 2/7 kg of salt. How much sugar and salt did Seth buy at the grocery store all together? Mark your answer.

A $\dfrac{3}{7}$ C $\dfrac{2}{7}$

B $\dfrac{1}{7}$ D $\dfrac{6}{7}$

Reporting Category 2 – 4.3 (F) Number and Operations

☐ **Prenilla makes 2 friendship bracelets. Her first bracelet took 8/12 of an hour to make. Her second bracelet took 5/12 of an hour to make. How much more time did the first bracelet take to make? Mark your answer.**

A $\dfrac{13}{12}$ C $\dfrac{1}{4}$

B $\dfrac{13}{24}$ D $\dfrac{1}{2}$

Reporting Category 2 – 4.3 (F) Number and Operations

☐ **Subtract the fractions and simplify your answers. Mark your answer.**

$$\frac{49}{32} - \frac{41}{32} = \square$$

A $\dfrac{90}{32}$ C $\dfrac{9}{8}$

B $\dfrac{1}{4}$ D $\dfrac{1}{2}$

Reporting Category 2 – 4.3 (F) Number and Operations

☐ **Add the fractions and simplify your answers. Mark your answer.**

$$\frac{21}{59} + \frac{26}{59} = \square$$

A $\dfrac{5}{59}$ C $\dfrac{47}{118}$

B $\dfrac{46}{59}$ D $\dfrac{47}{59}$

Reporting Category 2 – 4.3 (F) Number and Operations

□ Sylvester works at a pizza restaurant. He is making a cheese pizza for a customer. He used $\frac{3}{10}$ cups of mozzarella cheese and $\frac{6}{10}$ cups of cheddar cheese. How much cheese did Sylvester use all together on the pizza? Mark your answer.

A $\frac{9}{10}$ C $\frac{9}{20}$

B $\frac{3}{10}$ D $\frac{3}{4}$

Reporting Category 2 – 4.3 (F) Number and Operations

□ Add the fractions and simplify your answers. Mark your answer.

$$\frac{54}{81} + \frac{45}{81} = \square$$

A $\frac{1}{9}$ C $\frac{98}{81}$

B $\frac{99}{162}$ D $\frac{11}{9}$

Reporting Category 2 – 4.3 (F) Number and Operations

□ Subtract the fractions and simplify your answers. Mark your answer.

$$\frac{48}{72} - \frac{24}{72} = \square$$

A $\frac{26}{72}$ C $\frac{1}{3}$

B 1   D $\frac{71}{72}$

Reporting Category 2 – 4.4 (A) Number and Operations

☐ **The Fourth of July parade is Saturday. Mrs. Thomas believes many people will buy cookies from her bakery while at the parade. In order to get ready for Saturday, her bakery baked 456 cookies on Wednesday, 321 cookies on Thursday, and 478 cookies on Friday. How many cookies did she bake on those 3 days? Mark your answer.**

A   **1,145 cookies**

B   **1,355 cookies**

C   **1,255 cookies**

D   **1,265 cookies**

Reporting Category 2 – 4.4 (A) Number and Operations

☐ **Ms. Bateman bought an entertainment center that cost $1,042, a table that cost $599, and a sofa that cost $755. How much did she spend altogether, not including tax? Mark your answer.**

A   **$2,386**

B   **$1,386**

C   **$2,496**

D   **$2,396**

Reporting Category 2 – 4.4 (A) Number and Operations

☐ **A concert had 2,852 people in attendance on Friday, 4,199 people on Saturday, and 3,005 people on Sunday. What was the total number of people who attended the concert on those 3 days? Mark your answer.**

A   **9,946**

B   **10,056**

C   **10,066**

D   **10,156**

Reporting Category 2 – 4.4 (A) Number and Operations

☐ Charley's class collected 4,954 cans last year. If they collected 1,976 cans before January, how many cans were collected after January? Mark your answer.

A   3,978

B   6,930

C   2,978

D   3,088

Reporting Category 2 – 4.4 (A) Number and Operations

☐ The Lopez family went to Mexico on their vacation. They spent part of the time traveling in their car and the rest of the time traveling in an airplane. They traveled 2,175 miles in their car. What additional information is needed to find how many miles were traveled in an airplane? Mark your answer.

A   No additional information is needed.

B   The number of days they were gone

C   The total number of miles they traveled

D   The number of people in their family

Reporting Category 2 – 4.4 (A) Number and Operations

☐ Madison bought a new book that contains 250 pages. She has been reading it for 5 days and has 30 pages left until she finishes the book. Which shows the number of pages Madison has read in 5 days? Mark your answer.

A   250 + 30 + 5

B   250 ÷ 5

C   30 – 5

D   250 – 30

Name _____

Reporting Category 2 – 4.4 (A) Number and Operations

[ ] **Kathryn sold 74 tickets to an art exhibit. Jennifer sold 39 more tickets than Kathryn, and Faith sold 18 fewer tickets than Jennifer. How many tickets did Faith sell? Mark your answer.**

A   56

B   95

C   21

D   57

Reporting Category 2 – 4.4 (A) Number and Operations

[ ] **A school band had 468 members at the beginning of the school year. In September 79 members dropped out, but 125 new members joined the band in October. After the football season ended, 285 members left the band and enrolled in other activities. How many students were left in the band? Mark your answer.**

A   331

B   351

C   957

D   229

Reporting Category 2 – 4.4 (A) Number and Operations

[ ] **A new building was built in Dallas. It is 1,207 feet tall. The building next to it is 897 feet tall. If the buildings were stacked on top of each other, how tall would they be altogether? Mark your answer.**

A   1,094 ft

B   2,104 ft

C   2,004 ft

D   1,104 ft

Reporting Category 2 – 4.4 (A) Number and Operations

☐ A city in the United States has a population of 4,257,388. A city in Asia has a population of 7,125,210. How much larger is the city in Asia than the city in the United States? Mark your answer.

A   2,867,822

B   3,132,178

C   3,978,932

D   2,868,822

Reporting Category 2 – 4.4 (A) Number and Operations

☐ Mr. Murphy's grocery store sold 1,328 pounds of turkey during Thanksgiving. This was 449 pounds more than he sold last year. How many pounds of turkey did he sell last year? Mark your answer.

A   889 lbs

B   879 lbs

C   1,777 lbs

D   989 lbs

Reporting Category 2 – 4.4 (A) Number and Operations

☐ Mr. Aster took his scooter in for repairs. The mechanic told him the parts would cost $48, new paint would cost $25, and chrome trim would cost $28, plus the labor charges. What other information is needed to find the total cost for the repairs to the scooter? Mark your answer.

A   The cost of a new motor

B   The age of the scooter

C   The length of time to repair the scooter

D   The charges for labor

Name _____

Reporting Category 2 – 4.4 (A) Number and Operations

☐ Matthew had 632 baseball cards. He wanted to sell some of them so he could buy 50 action figures. He sold 238 of the baseball cards to a hobby store. Which shows the number of baseball cards Matthew did *not* sell? Mark your answer.

A   238 + 50

B   632 – 238

C   632 – 238 + 50

D   632 ÷ 238

Reporting Category 2 – 4.4 (A) Number and Operations

☐ Miss Watson has collected 123 autographs from famous musicians. Her older sister has collected 37 more autographs than Miss Watson, and Mason has collected 19 fewer autographs than Miss Watson's older sister. How many autographs does Mason have? Mark your answer.

A   18

B   104

C   179

D   141

Reporting Category 2 – 4.4 (A) Number and Operations

☐ Moffett Elementary purchased 500 envelopes in January. During February, 237 letters were sent to parents using the envelopes. In March, 79 letters were sent to parents. A total of 375 more envelopes were bought in April. How many envelopes does the school office now have? Mark your answer.

A   600

B   559

C   569

D   659

Reporting Category 2 – 4.4 (A) Number and Operations

☐ A fitness center keeps a record of the number of minutes members use the facility. Kim's mom has used the center for 327 minutes, and her dad has used the center for 254 minutes. Sara's mom joined the exercise center this month, so she has only used the center for 192 minutes. How many minutes have the 3 people spent at the exercise center? Mark your answer.

A   763 min

B   772 min

C   663 min

D   773 min

Reporting Category 2 – 4.4 (A) Number and Operations

☐ A third grade earned $1,448, a fourth grade earned $2,261, and a fifth grade earned $2,574 at a fall festival. How much did the 3 grades earn altogether at the fall festival? Mark your answer.

A $6,283

B $6,373

C $5,173

D $5,283

Reporting Category 2 – 4.4 (A) Number and Operations

☐ The Thomas family traveled 1,841 miles on a trip in July. In August they traveled 479 miles on another trip. How many miles did the family travel on the 2 trips? Mark your answer.

A   2,320 mi

B   1,210 mi

C   1,320 mi

D   2,310 mi

Reporting Category 2 – 4.4 (A) Number and Operations

☐ **Williams Elementary sponsored a magic show to raise money for the library. The fourth grade sold 175, the fifth grade sold 298, and the sixth grade sold 310 tickets. How many tickets were sold by the 3 grade levels? Mark your answer.**

A   793

B   783

C   683

D   673

Reporting Category 2 – 4.4 (A) Number and Operations

☐ **Andy's baseball team has hit 9 homeruns this season. Jared's team has hit 17 homeruns this season. Which expression could be used to find how many homeruns Andy's team needs to hit to tie with Jared's team? Mark your answer.**

A   17 – 9

B   9 + 17

C   17 × 9

D   17 ÷ 9

Reporting Category 2 – 4.4 (A) Number and Operations

☐ **Capital Elementary School has 257 girls and 310 boys in the fourth grade. Avenue C Elementary has 403 boys and 276 girls in the fourth grade. How many more boys attend Avenue C Elementary than Capital Elementary? Mark your answer.**

A   19

B   146

C   34

D   93

Reporting Category 2 – 4.4 (A) Number and Operations

☐ Ms. Sanchez bought some peanuts, 5 pounds of apples, 3 pounds of bananas, and 2 pounds of candy. She paid $5 for the peanuts. What other information is needed to find how many pounds of peanuts she bought? Mark your answer.

A   The cost of the peanuts per pound

B   How much she spent for the other items

C   No more information is needed.

D   How many pounds of peanuts Ms. Sanchez bought

Reporting Category 2 – 4.4 (A) Number and Operations

☐ A furniture store's web site has been visited by 2,234,351 people this year. A flooring company's web site has been visited by 2,256,230 people. How many fewer people have visited the furniture store's web site than the flooring company's web site? Mark your answer.

A   22,121

B   21,881

C   21,889

D   21,879

Reporting Category 2 – 4.4 (A) Number and Operations

☐ Mrs. Newsome earned $1,448 at her garage sale. Her sister earned $2,261 at her yard sale, and her son earned $2,574 at his estate sale. How much did the 3 family members earn altogether? Mark your answer.

A $5,173

B $6,373

C $6,283

D $5,283

Name _____

Reporting Category 2 – 4.4 (B) Number and Operations

☐ **In which number sentence does 9 make the equation true? Mark your answer.**

A $\boxed{} \div 27 = 3$

B $27 \times \boxed{} = 3$

C $\boxed{} \times 27 = 3$

D $27 \div \boxed{} = 3$

Reporting Category 2 – 4.4 (B) Number and Operations

☐ **Molly pasted 54 stamps in a stamp album. She pasted 6 stamps on each page. Which number sentence is in the same fact family as $54 \div 6 = \boxed{}$? Mark your answer.**

A $\boxed{} - 54 = 6$

B $6 \times 54 = \boxed{}$

C $\boxed{} \times 6 = 54$

D $6 + \boxed{} = 54$

Reporting Category 2 – 4.4 (B) Number and Operations

☐ **In which number sentence does 6 make the equation true? Mark your answer.**

A $56 \div \boxed{} = 8$

B $48 \div \boxed{} = 8$

C $64 \div \boxed{} = 8$

D $40 \div \boxed{} = 8$

Reporting Category 2 – 4.4 (B) Number and Operations

[ ] Which number sentence is NOT in the same fact family as 72 ÷ [ ] = 8? Mark your answer.

A   8 × [ ] = 72

B   72 ÷ 8 = [ ]

C   72 × [ ] = 8

D   [ ] × 8 = 72

Reporting Category 2 – 4.4 (B) Number and Operations

[ ] In which number sentence does 12 make the equation true? Mark your answer.

A   77 ÷ [ ] = 7

B   70 ÷ [ ] = 7

C   63 ÷ [ ] = 7

D   84 ÷ [ ] = 7

Reporting Category 2 – 4.4 (B) Number and Operations

[ ] Exactly 42 bottles of soda were placed on some shelves. There were 7 bottles on each shelf. Which number sentence is in the same fact family as 42 ÷ [ ] = 7? Mark your answer.

A   [ ] – 7 = 42

B   7 × 42 = [ ]

C   7 ÷ [ ] = 42

D   7 × [ ] = 42

Name _____

Reporting Category 2 – 4.4 (B) Number and Operations

☐ **William found 48 sea shells on the beach at Galveston. He put an equal number of shells in 6 boxes. Which number sentence is in the same fact family as 48 ÷ 6 = ☐ ? Mark your answer.**

A $48 \times \boxed{} = 6$

B $48 + 6 = \boxed{}$

C $48 \times 6 = \boxed{}$

D $\boxed{} \times 6 = 48$

Reporting Category 2 – 4.4 (B) Number and Operations

☐ **In which number sentence does 11 make the equation true? Mark your answer.**

A $\boxed{} \div 55 = 5$

B $5 \times 55 = \boxed{}$

C $55 \div \boxed{} = 5$

D $5 + \boxed{} = 55$

Reporting Category 2 – 4.4 (B) Number and Operations

☐ **In which number sentence does 5 make the equation true? Mark your answer.**

A $\boxed{} \div 30 = 6$

B $30 \div \boxed{} = 6$

C $6 \div \boxed{} = 30$

D $30 \times \boxed{} = 6$

Reporting Category 2 – 4.4 (B) Number and Operations

☐ Which number sentence is NOT in the same fact family as $9 \times \square = 63$? Mark your answer.

A $63 \div 9 = \square$

B $63 \div \square = 9$

C $\square \times 9 = 63$

D $63 \times 9 = \square$

Reporting Category 2 – 4.4 (B) Number and Operations

☐ Caroline and her mother baked 60 cookies for a school bake sale. She put 5 cookies in each bag to be sold. Which number sentence is in the same fact family as $60 \div 5 = \square$? Mark your answer.

A $5 \times \square = 60$

B $60 + 5 = \square$

C $60 \times 5 = \square$

D $\square \div 60 = 5$

Reporting Category 2 – 4.4 (B) Number and Operations

☐ In which number sentence does 7 make the equation true? Mark your answer.

A $63 \div \square = 8$

B $49 \div \square = 8$

C $56 \div \square = 8$

D $42 \div \square = 8$

Name _____

Reporting Category 2 – 4.4 (C) Number and Operations

☐ Avery arranged some pictures of animals in the pattern shown below. Which number sentence best represents Avery's pattern? Mark your answer.

A   3 + 4 = 7

B   3 + 9 = 12

C   3 × 4 = 12

D   3 × 3 = 9

Reporting Category 2 – 4.4 (C) Number and Operations

☐ Which of the following best represents the drawings? Mark your answer.

⬜⬜⬜   ⬜⬜⬜
⬜⬜⬜   ⬜⬜⬜
⬜⬜⬜   ⬜⬜⬜⬜

A   3 + 3 + 4 + 3   C   (3 × 3) + (4 × 3)

B   (3 + 3) × (4 + 3)   D   3 × (4 × 3)

Reporting Category 2 – 4.4 (C) Number and Operations

☐   or

2 × (2 + 4) is the same as which of the following number sentences? Mark your answer.

A   (2 + 2) × (2 + 4)

B   (2 + 2 + 4)

C   (2 × 4) × 2

D   (2 × 2) + (2 × 4)

Name _____

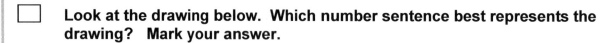

DIAGNOSTIC

Reporting Category 2 – 4.4 (C) Number and Operations

☐ Look at the drawing below. Which number sentence best represents the drawing?   Mark your answer.

A   5 × 2 = 10

B   5 × 2 = 2 × 5

C   2 + 5 + 5 + 2 = 14

D   2 + 5 = 5 + 2

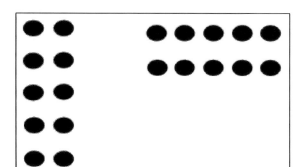

Reporting Category 2 – 4.4 (C) Number and Operations

☐ To find the number of cubes in the figure below.

you can place them like this:

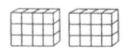

Which of the following is the same as (2 × 3) × 4? Mark your answer.

A

B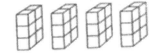

C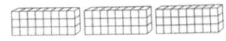

D

Reporting Category 2 – 4.4 (C) Number and Operations

Some arrays for the number 24 are shown below.

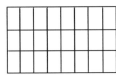

3 × 8

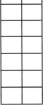

12 × 2   4 × 6

Which shows another array for the number 24? Mark your answer.

A

B

C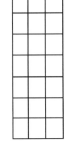

D

Reporting Category 2 – 4.4 (C) Number and Operations

Which number sentence does this drawing best represent?   Mark your answer.

A   20 ÷ 2 = 10

B   20 ÷ 4 = 5

C   2 + 2 + 2 + 2 + 2 = 10

D   10 × 2 = 20

Reporting Category 2 – 4.4 (C) Number and Operations

   or

2 × (3 + 6) is the same as which of the number sentences?   Mark your answer.

A   2 × (3 × 6)   C   (2 × 3) + (2 × 6)

B   (2 + 3) × (2 + 6)   D   2 + (3 + 6)

Reporting Category 2 – 4.4 (C) Number and Operations

Which of the following best represents the drawings?

☐ ☐ ☐ ☐ ☐ ☐   ☐ ☐ ☐ ☐
☐ ☐ ☐ ☐ ☐ ☐   ☐ ☐ ☐ ☐
                    ☐ ☐ ☐ ☐

A   (2 × 7) + (3 × 4)

B   (2 + 7) × (3 + 4)

C   2 + 7 + 3 + 4

D   (2 × 7) × (3 × 4)

Reporting Category 2 – 4.4 (C) Number and Operations

☐ **Which of the following best represents the drawings? Mark your answer.**

A   6 + 2 = 4 + 3

B   (2 × 12) = (3 × 12)

C   2 + 6 + 4 = 12

D   6 × 2 = 4 × 3

Reporting Category 2 – 4.4 (C) Number and Operations

☐ **To find the number of cubes in the figure below.**

you can place them like this:

Which of the following is the same as (2 × 3) × 6? Mark your answer.

A   C

B 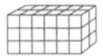   D

Reporting Category 2 – 4.4 (C) Number and Operations

☐ **Which number sentence does this drawing best represent? Mark your answer.**

A $(6 + 4) \times 3 = 6 \times (4 + 3)$

B $(6 \times 4) + 3 = 6 + (4 \times 3)$

C $(6 \times 4) \times 3 = 6 \times (4 \times 3)$

D $(6 - 4) \times 3 = 6 - (4 \times 3)$

Reporting Category 2 – 4.4 (C) Number and Operations

☐ **Which number sentence does the picture best represent? Mark your answer.**

A $4 \div 2 = 2$

B $2 \times 4 = 4 \times 2$

C $2 + 4 = 4 + 2$

D $8 - 4 = 4$

Reporting Category 2 – 4.4 (C) Number and Operations

☐ **Which of the following best represents the drawing? Mark your answer.**

A $(4 + 3) \times (2 + 4)$

B $4 \times 3 \times 2$

C $4 + 3 + 2 + 4$

D $(4 \times 3) + (2 \times 4)$

Name _____

ASSESSMENT

Reporting Category 2 – 4.4 (C) Number and Operations

☐ **Which number sentence does this drawing best represent? Mark your answer.**

A   (10 × 3) + 2 = 10 × (3 + 2)

B   (10 − 3) × 2 = 10 − (3 × 2)

C   (10 × 3) ÷ 2 = 10 × (3 ÷ 2)

D   (10 × 3) × 2 = 10 × (3 × 2)

Reporting Category 2 – 4.4 (C) Number and Operations

☐ **Which of the following is the same as (3 × 3) × 2? Mark your answer.**

A   C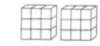

B   D

Reporting Category 2 – 4.4 (C) Number and Operations

☐ **Ava found a group of hats in the garage. She arranged them in the pattern shown below. Which number sentence best represents Ava's pattern? Mark your answer.**

A   5 + 2 = 7   C   (5 + 5) × 2 = 20

B   2 × 5 = 10   D   2 × 6 = 12

© Teachers' Treasures Publishing

Page 101

Reporting Category 2 – 4.4 (C) Number and Operations

 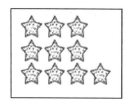   or

2 × (3 + 3 + 4) is the same as which of the following number sentences? Mark your answer.

A   (2 × 3) + (2 × 3) + (2 × 4)

B   (3 + 3 + 3 + 3) × (2 × 4)

C   (2 + 3) + (2 + 3) + (2 + 4)

D   2 + (3 × 3 × 4)

Reporting Category 2 – 4.4 (C) Number and Operations

Which number sentence best represents the drawing below? Mark your answer.

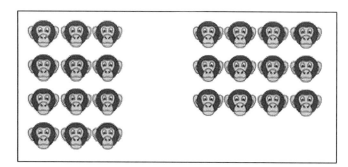

A   4 + 3 = 3 + 4

B   12 × 12

C   4 × 3 = 3 × 4

D   4 × 3 + 3 × 4

Reporting Category 2 – 4.4 (D) Number and Operations

☐ During one month Christian brought pencils for his classmates 13 times. There were 20 school days in the month and 27 students in his class. How many pencils did Christian bring to school during the month? Mark your answer.

A 40

B 540

C 60

D 351

Reporting Category 2 – 4.4 (D) Number and Operations

☐ Connor saves his allowance. He receives $15 a week for doing chores for his family. How much money will he save in 9 weeks? Mark your answer.

A $24

B $135

C $95

D $145

Reporting Category 2 – 4.4 (D) Number and Operations

☐ What information is needed to solve the following problem? Mark your answer.

Arin slept 9 hours every night when she stayed with her grandparents last summer. How many hours did she sleep altogether?

A The time she went to bed each night and woke up each morning

B The number of times Arin has visited her grandparents

C The number of days Arin spent at her grandparents

D No more information is needed.

Reporting Category 2 – 4.4 (D) Number and Operations

☐ **William, Sebastian, and Emily ordered 2 large sausage pizzas and 3 large cheese pizzas for a party. The large pizzas each cost $9. Which method could be used to find the total cost of the order? Mark your answer.**

A   Add $9 to the sum of 2 and 3

B   Add 2 and 3, multiply by $9

C   Subtract 3 from $9, multiply by 2

D   Multiply 2 and 3, add $9

Reporting Category 2 – 4.4 (D) Number and Operations

☐ **David earned $15 for caring for his neighbor's cats one weekend. Anna earned $5.35 for each dog she took care of during a weekend. How much more did Anna earn than David if she cared for 3 dogs during the weekend? Mark your answer.**

A $9.65

B $16.05

C $31.05

D $1.05

Reporting Category 2 – 4.4 (D) Number and Operations

☐ **It is said 1 human year is equal to 7 years for a dog. Mason's dog had puppies on his 9th birthday. Which number sentence shows how to find how old the puppies will be in dog years when Mason is 14 years old? Mark your answer.**

A $9 \times (14 - 7) = 63$

B $9 \times (1 + 7) = 72$

C $(14 - 9) \times 7 = 35$

D $14 \times (14 - 7) = 98$

Reporting Category 2 – 4.4 (D) Number and Operations

☐ The chart gives the cost for a year's subscription for 4 different magazines. How much will a 15 year subscription to "Technology Plus" cost? Mark your answer.

A $60

B $51

C $440

D $540

Magazine	Cost of Subscription
Home Edition	$30
Technology Plus	$36
Hunters' Guide	$25
Food and Family	$25

Reporting Category 2 – 4.4 (D) Number and Operations

☐ Riley's mother baked 25 pans of cookies to sell at a school carnival. There were 36 cookies on each pan. How many cookies did she bake for the carnival? Mark your answer.

A   900

B   71

C   800

D   899

Reporting Category 2 – 4.4 (D) Number and Operations

☐ Khloe has been running for 3 months trying to earn a place on the girls' track team. She runs 4 miles each day after school and rests on the weekends. Which method could be used to find the total number of miles she will run in 15 days? Mark your answer.

A   Add 3 and 4, multiply by 15

B   Multiply 15 by 4

C   Subtract 3 from 4, multiply by 15

D   Add 3, 4, and 15

Reporting Category 2 – 4.4 (D) Number and Operations

☐ **What information is needed to solve the following problem? Mark your answer.**

> The fourth grade classes at Moore Intermediate had a raffle for a skateboard. Each of the students was given 25 tickets to sell. How many tickets were sold?

A   The number of students in the fourth grade

B   The price of each raffle ticket

C   The number of fourth grade classes

D   No more information is needed.

Reporting Category 2 – 4.4 (D) Number and Operations

☐ **Cameron had $29 and his sister had $18 in pennies. Which number sentence could be used to find the total number of pennies they had altogether? Mark your answer.**

A $(29 + 18) \times 100$

B $100 + (29 + 18)$

C $(29 + 18) + 100$

D $(29 \times 18) - 100$

Reporting Category 2 – 4.4 (D) Number and Operations

☐ **Payton bought 68 stamps for his new stamp book. The book has 15 pages, and he can put 6 stamps on each page. How many more stamps does he need to buy to fill all of the pages in his new stamp book? Mark your answer.**

A   158 stamps

B   90 stamps

C   22 stamps

D   32 stamps

Name _____

Reporting Category 2 – 4.4 (D) Number and Operations

☐ For 2 hours Katelyn has been helping her teacher organize the library books in the classroom. Katelyn made 16 stacks of books with 7 books in each stack. Which method could be used to find the total number of library books in the 16 stacks? Mark your answer.

A   Subtract 7 from 16, add 2

B   Add 16 and 7, multiply by 2

C   Multiply 16 by 7

D   Add 2, 16, 16, and 7

Reporting Category 2 – 4.4 (D) Number and Operations

☐ Miguel's mother needed to go to a store. She told him she would return in 15 minutes. While she was gone, Miguel filled 13 boxes with old magazines. Each box held 29 magazines. How many magazines did Miguel pack while his mother was gone? Mark your answer.

A   5,655

B   42

C   377

D   57

Reporting Category 2 – 4.4 (D) Number and Operations

☐ What information is needed to solve the following problem? Mark your answer.

> Sean helped his father unpack 45 cases of green beans at his father's grocery store. How many cans of green beans did Sean and his father unpack?

A   The number of cases delivered to the store

B   The number of cans in each case

C   The number of cans Brandon unpacked

D   No more information is needed.

Reporting Category 2 – 4.4 (D) Number and Operations

☐ Grace's mother made 7 flower beds in the front yard. She wants to plant 23 bushes in each bed. How many bushes will she plant in the front yard? Mark your answer.

A   16

B   161

C   30

D   3

Reporting Category 2 – 4.4 (D) Number and Operations

☐ Hayden has $30 in the bank. Every month his grandmother gives him $9 to put in his account. His sister has $44 in the bank. Every month her grandfather gives her $8 to put in her account. How much more money will his sister have than Hayden in 6 months? Mark your answer.

A $11

B $8

C $6

D $176

Reporting Category 2 – 4.4 (D) Number and Operations

☐ A pass to ride a city bus costs $0.75 for regular hours and $1.50 during rush hours. Mrs. French wants to buy 7 regular passes and 9 rush hour passes. Which number sentence could she use to find how much money she will spend?   Mark your answer.

A   (75¢ × 7) × ($1.50 × 9)

B   (75¢ × 7) + ($1.50 × 9)

C   (75¢ × 9) + ($1.50 × 7)

D   (75¢ + 7) × ($1.59 + 9)

Reporting Category 2 – 4.4 (D) Number and Operations

☐ **Forest Hills Elementary has 18 fourth grade classrooms. Each classroom needs 25 desks and 4 reading tables. The custodians need to have the classrooms ready in 5 days. Which method could be used to find the total number of desks needed for all of the fourth grade classrooms? Mark your answer.**

A   **Multiply 18 by 25**

B   **Multiply 18 by 25, add 4 and 5**

C   **Add 18 and 25**

D   **Multiply 25 by 4, add 18**

Reporting Category 2 – 4.4 (D) Number and Operations

☐ **Jared has collected baseball cards for 5 years. He has 37 boxes with 75 cards in each box. How many baseball cards has Jared collected? Mark your answer.**

A   **375**

B   **2,775**

C   **185**

D   **560**

Reporting Category 2 – 4.4 (D) Number and Operations

☐ **The chart shows the sales in dollars Hebert's Seafood Company made in a month. If the sales remain the same for the next 36 months, how much money will the company make? Mark your answer.**

A   **$340**

B   **$12,240**

C   **$376**

D   **$1,020**

Kind of Seafood	Sales in Dollars
Lobster	$99
Halibut	$104
Shrimp	$78
Crab	$59

Reporting Category 2 – 4.4 (D) Number and Operations

☐ Mr. Baker bought 23 shrubs to plant in a city park. There are 11 flower beds in the park. If he plants 8 shrubs in each flower bed, how many more shrubs does he need to buy? Mark your answer.

A 65

B 88

C 4

D 184

Reporting Category 2 – 4.4 (D) Number and Operations

☐ Isabella saved 15 quarters and 7 half dollars during one month. Which number sentence could she use to find how much money she has saved? Mark your answer.

A (15 × 7) + (50 × 25)

B (15 + 25) + (50 + 7)

C (15 × 25 × 50 × 7)

D (15 × 25) + (50 × 7)

Reporting Category 2 – 4.4 (D) Number and Operations

☐ What information is needed to solve the following problem? Mark your answer.

> Andrew has a paper route. A subscription to the newspaper costs $28 per month. What is the total amount of money he earns in a month?

A The number of hours it takes him to throw the papers

B The number of days he delivers the papers

C The number of papers he throws

D No more information is needed.

Name _____

Reporting Category 2 – 4.4 (E) Number and Operations

☐ A florist delivered 30 flower arrangements on Friday. The arrangements cost $15 each. Each arrangement held 25 flowers. Which number sentence could be used to find the total number of flowers used in the arrangements? Mark your answer.

A   30 + $15 = ☐

B   25 × 30 × $15 = ☐

C   30 × 25 = ☐

D   30 ÷ $15 = ☐

Reporting Category 2 – 4.4 (E) Number and Operations

☐ Eric had 92 pennies. He put them into 8 boxes. If he put the same number of pennies in each box, which number sentence could be used to find the number of pennies in each box? Mark your answer.

A   92 + 8 = ☐

B   92 × 8 = ☐

C   92 − 8 = ☐

D   92 ÷ 8 = ☐

Reporting Category 2 – 4.4 (E) Number and Operations

☐ Mrs. Baker canned 40 cans of tomatoes last summer. She put the same number of cans on each shelf. Which arrangement would NOT be possible if she put all of the cans of tomatoes on the shelves? Mark your answer.

A   5 shelves of 8 cans

B   4 shelves of 10 cans

C   8 shelves of 6 cans

D   2 shelves of 20 cans

Reporting Category 2 – 4.4 (E) Number and Operations

☐ A factory made 1,500 footballs over a period of 15 days. If the same number of footballs were made each day, which number sentence could be used to find how many footballs were made in one day? Mark your answer.

A $1,500 + 15 = \Box$

B $1,500 \div 15 = \Box$

C $1,500 - 15 = \Box$

D $1,500 \times 15 = \Box$

Reporting Category 2 – 4.4 (E) Number and Operations

☐ Luke found 22 seashells on a beach. His brothers found 3 times as many as he did. Which number sentence could be used to find the number of seashells his brothers found? Mark your answer.

A $\Box \div 3 = 22$

B $22 + 3 = \Box$

C $22 - \Box = 3$

D $22 \times 3 = \Box$

Reporting Category 2 – 4.4 (E) Number and Operations

☐ There are 14 fourth grade classes and 11 third grade classes at Brooks Intermediate. Each fourth grade class has 24 students. Which number sentence could be used to find the total number of students in the fourth grade? Mark your answer.

A $14 + 11 + 24 = \Box$

B $14 \times 24 = \Box$

C $24 \div 14 = \Box$

D $11 \times 24 = \Box$

Name _____

Reporting Category 2 – 4.4 (E) Number and Operations

☐ A hobby club meets 20 times a year. The 35 members pay $22 a year in dues to belong to the club. Which number sentence could be used to find the total amount of money paid in dues for a year? Mark your answer.

A   35 + $22 = ☐

B   20 × $22 = ☐

C   35 + $22 + 20 = ☐

D   35 × $22 = ☐

Reporting Category 2 – 4.4 (E) Number and Operations

☐ A baseball team scored 56 points during the summer season. If they scored the same number of points in each game, which of the following would NOT be possible? Mark your answer,

A   7 games with 8 points

B   18 games with 3 points

C   14 games with 4 points

D   28 games with 2 points

Reporting Category 2 – 4.4 (E) Number and Operations

☐ Christopher gets $5 a week for his allowance. When he is 16 years old, he will get 5 times as much for his allowance. Which number sentence could be used to find how much money Christopher will get for his allowance when he is 16?

A   5 + 5 = 10

B   5 × 5 = 25

C   5 + 16 = 21

D   16 + 5 + 5 = 26

Name _____

Reporting Category 2 – 4.4 (E) Number and Operations

☐   A snow cone stand is open 7 days a week.   Last week it sold 88 snow cones each day. Which number sentence could be used to find the number of snow cones sold last week? Mark your answer.

A   88 ÷ 7 = ☐

B   88 + 7 = ☐

C   88 × 7 = ☐

D   88 − 7 = ☐

Reporting Category 2 – 4.4 (E) Number and Operations

☐   A bread truck makes deliveries to Maples Market 4 days each week. On each delivery the store receives 54 loaves of bread. Which number sentence could be used to find the number of loaves of bread delivered in 3 weeks? Mark your answer.

A   54 × 4 ÷ 3

B   54 × 4 × 3

C   54 + 4 + 3

D   54 ÷ (4 + 3)

Reporting Category 2 – 4.4 (E) Number and Operations

☐   Twelve measuring cups were filled with pancake batter. Each cup held 3 cups of batter. Which number sentence represents the total amount of pancake batter in the cups? Mark your answer.

A   12 − 3 = 9

B   12 + 3 = 15

C   12 × 3 = 36

D   12 ÷ 3 = 4

Reporting Category 2 – 4.4 (F) Number and Operations

☐ Dat's mother made favors for his birthday party. She put 675 small pieces of candy into 9 bags. If she put the same amount of candy in each bag, how many pieces were in each bag? Mark your answer.

A   85

B   75

C   691

D   6,075

Reporting Category 2 – 4.4 (F) Number and Operations

☐ What is the remainder when 62 is divided by 8? Mark your answer.

A   54

B   70

C   7

D   6

Reporting Category 2 – 4.4 (F) Number and Operations

☐ Carlita volunteered to bring sodas for a class party. There are 29 students in her class including herself. There are 8 sodas in each carton. What is the smallest number of cartons Carlita should bring for the party? Mark your answer.

A   37

B   3

C   4

D   21

Reporting Category 2 – 4.4 (F) Number and Operations

☐ **What information is needed to solve the following problem? Mark your answer.**

> **Mr. Ramirez bought fencing for his yard. He needs to cut it into 9 equal pieces. He will have 3 feet left over when he finishes the job. How long will each piece of fencing be?**

A   Where Mr. Ramirez will place the fencing

B   How much the fencing cost per foot

C   How much fencing he bought

D   No more information is needed.

Reporting Category 2 – 4.4 (F) Number and Operations

☐ **Evan has read 10 books this year. He wants to finish a 70 page book in one week. Which number sentence shows how many pages he will need to read each day if he reads the same amount of pages each day? Mark your answer.**

A 10×70 C $70 \div 10$

B $10 \div 7$ D $70 \div 7$

Reporting Category 2 – 4.4 (F) Number and Operations

☐ **What do you need to do to solve this problem? Mark your answer.**

> **Brandon wants to buy tires for his three-wheeler. The tires will cost a total of $27. How much will 1 tire cost?**

A   Divide $27 by 3

B   Divide $27 by 4

C   Add $27 and 3

D   Multiply $27 by 3

Name _____

Reporting Category 2 – 4.4 (F) Number and Operations

☐ Luis charges $15 for mowing a lawn. He wants to earn $45 to buy a new tank for his fish. Which number sentence could be used to find how many lawns he must mow to earn $45? Mark your answer.

A $45 \div 15 = \square$

B $60 \div 15 = \square$

C $45 - 15 = \square$

D $45 \times 15 = \square$

Reporting Category 2 – 4.4 (F) Number and Operations

☐ The game Match Spot has 104 tiles. When Zachary and his friends played the game, each person received an equal number of tiles. What other information is needed to determine the number of tiles each person had? Mark your answer.

A   The total number of players

B   The score of each player in the game

C   The total number of tiles in the game

D   No more information is needed.

Reporting Category 2 – 4.4 (F) Number and Operations

☐ Mr. Zamora bought 28 shrubs to plant at his new house. He wanted to plant an equal number of shrubs in 6 different flowerbeds. When he finished planting the shrubs, he had 4 left over. How many shrubs did he plant in each flowerbed? Mark your answer.

A   3

B   4

C   5

D   6

Reporting Category 2 – 4.4 (F) Number and Operations

☐ **What is the remainder when 19 is divided by 4? Mark your answer.**

A   3

B   4

C   5

D   23

Reporting Category 2 – 4.4 (F) Number and Operations

☐ **Chase has collected 616 pennies he wants to put into 4 different piggy banks. If he puts the same amount of pennies in each bank, how many pennies will be in each bank? Mark your answer.**

A   612

B   2,464

C   154

D   620

Reporting Category 2 – 4.4 (F) Number and Operations

☐ **What do you need to do to solve this problem? Mark your answer.**

> Mr. Espinosa gave some of the students in his class 3 pencils each for perfect attendance. If he passed out a total of 36 pencils, how many students had perfect attendance?

A   Subtract 3 from 36

B   Divide 36 by 3

C   Add 36 and 3

D   Multiply 36 by 3

Reporting Category 2 – 4.4 (F) Number and Operations

☐ Bailey bought 3 bags of oranges and 2 bags of apples. The oranges cost $1.50, and the apples cost $0.98. Which number sentence could be used to find how much each bag of oranges cost? Mark your answer.

A $1.50 × 3 = ☐

B $1.50 ÷ 3 = ☐

C $1.50 + 3 = ☐

D $0.98 ÷ 3 = ☐

Reporting Category 2 – 4.4 (F) Number and Operations

☐ Layla wants to buy a new video game. The recycling center pays 30¢ per pound for cans. What other information is needed to determine the number of pounds she needs to collect to have enough money to buy the video game? Mark your answer.

A   The weight of the cans she collects

B   The number of bags of cans she will turn in to the recycling center

C   How long she will collect the cans

D   The cost of the video game

Reporting Category 2 – 4.4 (F) Number and Operations

☐ What is the remainder when 43 is divided by 5? Mark your answer.

A   2

B   3

C   48

D   4

Reporting Category 2 – 4.4 (F) Number and Operations

☐ **If 880 books are placed on 8 shelves in the library and each shelf has the same number of books on it, how many books are on each shelf? Mark your answer.**

A   772

B   111

C   7,040

D   110

Reporting Category 2 – 4.4 (F) Number and Operations

☐ **What do you need to do to solve this problem? Mark your answer.**

> Lauren gave each of her sisters 9 pieces of gum. Each package of gum contained 6 pieces of gum. If she gave away a total of 36 pieces of gum, how many sisters does Lauren have?

A   Divide 36 by 6

B   Divide 36 by 15

C   Divide 36 by 9

D   Multiply 36 by 6

Reporting Category 2 – 4.4 (F) Number and Operations

☐ **Carlos brought 46 cookies to school to share with his classmates. He gave each of 9 classmates an equal number of the cookies and had 1 cookie left over. How many cookies did he give to each classmate? Mark your answer.**

A   2

B   3

C   5

D   4

Reporting Category 2 – 4.4 (F) Number and Operations

☐ On Mia's birthday she invited some friends to a movie. Each ticket cost $2.50. She had $23.00 to pay for the tickets. What is the greatest number of friends she could invite to go to the movie with her? Mark your answer.

A   8

B   9

C   10

D   11

Reporting Category 2 – 4.4 (F) Number and Operations

☐ Alexander has 162 model cars he wants to store in 9 boxes. If he puts an equal number of cars in each box, how many cars will be in each box? Mark your answer.

A   19

B   10

C   18

D   9

Reporting Category 2 – 4.4 (F) Number and Operations

☐ One hundred eighty fourth grade students attended a play in a school auditorium. They sat on the first rows of seats. What other information is needed to determine the number of students on each row? Mark your answer.

A   The total number of seats in the auditorium

B   The total number of rows sat in by the fourth grade students

C   The total number of students in the fourth grade

D   The total number of students who attended the play

Reporting Category 2 – 4.4 (F) Number and Operations

☐ **What do you need to do to solve this problem? Mark your answer.**

> **Ella is organizing one of her 3 photo albums. The album contains 7 pages, and she has one hundred sixty-one pictures to place in it. If she places the same number of photos on a page, how many photos will she be able to place on each page?**

A   **Multiply 161 by 7**

B   **Divide 7 by 161**

C   **Divide 161 by 10**

D   **Divide 161 by 7**

Reporting Category 2 – 4.4 (F) Number and Operations

☐ **What is the remainder when 91 is divided by 6? Mark your answer.**

A   5

B   2

C   1

D   546

Reporting Category 2 – 4.4 (F) Number and Operations

☐ **Mrs. Morris brought chairs to a meeting. She put the chairs in 10 rows. If 69 attendees will sit in the chairs, what is the least number of chairs she put in each row so that each row had the same number of chairs? Mark your answer.**

A   6

B   3

C   7

D   5

Reporting Category 2 – 4.4 (G) Number and Operations

If Bella spends an average of 210 hours per month sleeping, about how many hours does she sleep in 5 days? Mark your answer.

A   205 hours

B   10 hours

C   40 hours

D   1,050 hours

Reporting Category 2 – 4.4 (G) Number and Operations

Ashley spends 48 to 52 minutes a day practicing her ballet dancing. Which is a reasonable total number of minutes she will practice her ballet dancing in 8 days? Mark your answer.

A   600 min

B   400 min

C   450 min

D   300 min

Reporting Category 2 – 4.4 (G) Number and Operations

Bus #10 travels 27 to 33 miles every day to Benjamin's school. Which is a reasonable total number of miles the bus travels in 20 days? Mark your answer.

A   Less than 300

B   Between 300 and 400

C   Between 400 and 500

D   More than 500

Reporting Category 2 – 4.4 (G) Number and Operations

☐ Miguel made miniature kites to sell in his mother's craft booth at a fair. Each kite had an 8 inch long ribbon tail. He had 244 inches of ribbon. Which is a reasonable total for the number of kites he made using 244 inches of ribbon? Mark your answer.

A   488

B   40

C   20

D   30

Reporting Category 2 – 4.4 (G) Number and Operations

☐ Mrs. Stevens drives 29 to 33 miles a day from her house to her job. Which is a reasonable total number of miles she will drive in 11 days? Mark your answer.

A   330 mi

B   250 mi

C   420 mi

D   370 mi

Reporting Category 2 – 4.4 (G) Number and Operations

☐ The fourth grade classes at Branch Intermediate are selling cookies to raise money for new gym equipment. If a class has 22 students and they each bring 2 dozen cookies, about how many cookies will the class sell? Mark your answer.

A   46 cookies

B   100 cookies

C   400 cookies

D   600 cookies

Reporting Category 2 – 4.4 (G) Number and Operations

☐ Mariah's mother is baking chocolate chip cookies for the fall festival. She plans to bake 15 dozen cookies. She needs 1 package of chocolate chips for each 2 dozen cookies. About how many packages of chocolate chips will she need to buy? Mark your answer.

A 7 packages

B 8 packages

C 15 packages

D 30 packages

Reporting Category 2 – 4.4 (G) Number and Operations

☐ If a school van can carry 18 passengers in one trip, which is a reasonable number of passengers the van can carry in 31 trips? Mark your answer.

A Less than 620

B Between 620 and 680

C Between 680 and 740

D More than 740

Reporting Category 2 – 4.4 (G) Number and Operations

☐ Tyrone has been saving his allowance for 5 weeks to buy a bicycle. If he saved between $3 and $6 each week, which is a reasonable total amount he has saved so far? Mark your answer.

A Between $12 and $35

B Between $15 and $25

C Less than $10

D Between $20 and $50

Reporting Category 2 – 4.4 (G) Number and Operations

☐ **Mr. Young bought 52 rose bushes to plant in his garden. He can plant 7 bushes on each row. About how many rows does he need to make for the rose bushes? Mark your answer.**

A   8

B   7

C   364

D   45

Reporting Category 2 – 4.4 (G) Number and Operations

☐ **About 781 airplanes have landed at a new airport during its first year. If the same number of planes land for the next 2 years, about how many planes will have landed since the airport opened? Mark your answer.**

A   1,600

B   2,400

C   1,562

D   1,000

Reporting Category 2 – 4.4 (G) Number and Operations

☐ **It takes Anna 36 to 42 minutes to ride her bicycle to school and back home every day. Which is a reasonable total number of minutes she spends riding her bicycle in 18 days? Mark your answer.**

A   Less than 100

B   Between 100 and 500

C   Between 500 and 1,000

D   More than 1,000

Reporting Category 2 – 4.4 (H) Number and Operations

[ ] **Liam's last four math pop quizzes totaled 363. Which answer best describes the result of finding his score? Mark your answer.**

A   Dividing 363 by 4 gives no remainder left.

B   Dividing 363 by 4 gives a remainder greater than 5.

C   Dividing 363 by 4 gives a remainder that is less than 4.

D   Dividing 363 by 4 gives a remainder that is more than 9.

Reporting Category 2 – 4.4 (H) Number and Operations

[ ] **Which of the following division equations has largest remainder left over? Mark your answer.**

A   1205 ÷ 120

B   1206 ÷ 120

C   1207 ÷ 120

D   1208 ÷ 120

Reporting Category 2 – 4.4 (H) Number and Operations

[ ] **If 198 = 19 × 10 + 8, which statement below is true? Mark your answer.**

A   Dividing 198 by 19 gives the remainder 10.

B   Dividing 198 by 19 gives the remainder 8.

C   Dividing 198 by 10 gives the remainder 19.

D   Dividing198 by 8 gives the remainder 10.

Reporting Category 2 – 4.4 (H) Number and Operations

☐ There are 10 centimeters in one decimeter, and 10 decimeters in 1 meter. How many centimeters are in 3.4 meters? Mark your answer.

A   34

B   340

C   3400

D   340.5

Reporting Category 2 – 4.4 (H) Number and Operations

☐ Which pair of division equations below have the same remainder? Mark your answer.

A $559 \div 19$ and $538 \div 19$

B $554 \div 19$ and $536 \div 19$

C $554 \div 19$ and $535 \div 19$

D $536 \div 19$ and $535 \div 19$

Reporting Category 2 – 4.4 (H) Number and Operations

☐ Mrs. LaRosa earned $2700 each month for the first three months of the year. She also earned $2800 each month for the following three months. How much did she earn during the first six months of the year? Mark your answer.

A $22,600

B $22,400

C $21,000

D $16,500

Reporting Category 2 – 4.4 (H) Number and Operations

[ ] The volume of a cube is calculated by multiplying length × width × height. The dimensions for a water reservoir are 120 ft, 40 ft, and 42 ft. Which is the volume of the reservoir?   Mark your answer.

A   201,600 cubic feet

B   221,600 cubic feet

C   222,400 cubic feet

D   224,600 cubic feet

Reporting Category 2 – 4.4 (H) Number and Operations

[ ] If there are 12 inches in one foot, and 3 feet in one yard, how many feet are in 6 yards and 132 inches? Mark your answer.

A   29 feet

B   27 feet

C   23 feet

D   21 feet

Reporting Category 2 – 4.4 (H) Number and Operations

[ ] Each pint of paint costs $0.45. There are 8 pints in one gallon.   If Jerald paid $18 for a bucket of paint, how many gallons of paint are in the bucket? Mark your answer.

A   14

B   12

C   5

D   3

Reporting Category 2 – 4.4 (H) Number and Operations

☐ **Jerry's Sporting Goods Store earnings for 2010-2013 are as follows:**

$64,800 in 2010
$32,008 every six months in 2011
$15,430 every three months in 2012
$5,100 per month in 2013

Which year had the highest monthly income? Mark your answer.

A   2010

B   2011

C   2012

D   2013

Reporting Category 2 – 4.4 (H) Number and Operations

☐ **Taylor teaches Piano classes for different rates based on the number weeks as described below.   Which option costs more than the others per student? Mark your answer.**

A $42 per student for each week for 10-week session

B $48 per student for each week for 8-week session

C $62 per student for each week for 6-week session

D $76 per student for each week for 5-week session

Reporting Category 2 – 4.4 (H) Number and Operations

☐ **If 1931 = 7 × 275 + 6 and 275 = 5 × 55. Subtracting which number below from 1931 allows us to divide it by 7, and then divide the result by 55 again without having a remainder? Mark your answer.**

A   6

B   8

C   9

D   11

Reporting Category 2 – 4.5 (A) Algebraic Reasoning

☐ A florist delivered 10 flower arrangements containing a total of 50 flowers. Which of the following could be *x*, the number of flowers in each arrangement? Mark your answer.

$$10 \times x = 50$$

A   50

B   10

C   5

D   40

Reporting Category 2 – 4.5 (A) Algebraic Reasoning

☐ A factory made the same number of footballs over a period of 15 days. If the factory made 10 footballs each day, which of the following could be *y*, the number of footballs made by the factory? Mark your answer.

$$y \div 15 = 10$$

A   25

B   5

C   1500

D   150

Reporting Category 2 – 4.5 (A) Algebraic Reasoning

☐ In Mrs. Barrow's class 5 students read 73 pages each. Which number sentence could be used to find *n*, the number of pages read in all? Mark your answer.

A $73 + 5 = n$

B $73 \times 5 = n$

C $73 \div 5 = n$

D $73 - n = 5$

Reporting Category 2 – 4.5 (A) Algebraic Reasoning

☐ A football team scored 31 points per game for each of 7 games. Which of the following could be *p*, the number of total points scored? Mark your answer.

$$p \div 7 = 31$$

A   38

B   217

C   108

D   24

Reporting Category 2 – 4.5 (A) Algebraic Reasoning

☐ Ms. Rogers canned tomatoes from her garden last summer. For 7 days she canned 34 cans of tomatoes each day. Which number sentence could be used to find *t*, the number of cans of tomatoes Ms. Rogers canned in all? Mark your answer.

A $34 \times 7 = t$

B $34 \div t = 7$

C $t - 7 = 34$

D $34 + 7 = t$

Reporting Category 2 – 4.5 (A) Algebraic Reasoning

☐ Members of a hobby club each pay $5 a year in dues. Which of the following could be *d*, the number of members if the club collected $90 in dues? Mark your answer.

$$\$5 \times d = \$90$$

A   85

B   450

C   95

D   18

Reporting Category 2 – 4.5 (A) Algebraic Reasoning

☐ A baseball team scored 8 runs in each of their last 14 games. Which number sentence could be used to find *r*, the number of runs scored in all? Mark your answer.

A $8 + 14 = r$

B $14 - r = 8$

C $14 \times 8 = r$

D $14 \div r = 8$

Reporting Category 2 – 4.5 (A) Algebraic Reasoning

☐ There are 9 fourth grade classes at Brooks Intermediate. Each class has the same number of students. If there are 216 students in the fourth grade, which of the following could be *s*, the number of students in each fourth grade class? Mark your answer.

$$9 \times s = 216$$

A   34

B   207

C   24

D   35

Reporting Category 2 – 4.5 (A) Algebraic Reasoning

☐ A music club sold 55 apples each day for 9 days. Which of the following could be *m*, the total number of apples sold? Mark your answer.

$$m \div 9 = 55$$

A   495

B   455

C   46

D   185

Reporting Category 2 – 4.5 (B) Algebraic Reasoning

☐ Goody Candy Company sells candy by the bag. The table below shows the number of bags and the number of pieces of candy in the bags.

Number of Bags	Number of Candy Pieces
2	200
5	500
9	900

Which correctly describes the relationship in the table? Mark your answer.

A   Number of bags × 10 = number of candy pieces

B   Number of bags × 100 = number of candy pieces

C   Number of bags + 198 = number of candy pieces

D   Number of bags + 16 = number of candy pieces

Reporting Category 2 – 4.5 (B) Algebraic Reasoning

☐ Each number in Set B is related in the same way to the number beside it in Set C.

Set B	Set C
4	24
10	60
7	42
40	240

When given a number in Set B, what is one way to find its related number in Set C? Mark your answer.

A   Add 20

B   Multiply by 7

C   Divide by 6

D   Multiply by 6

Reporting Category 2 – 4.5 (B) Algebraic Reasoning

☐ The table below shows how long it takes Drew and his friends to fold and wrap newspapers.

Number of Newspapers	20	15	120	30
Number of Minutes	4	3	24	6

What is one way to find the number of minutes it takes the boys to fold and wrap 10 newspapers? Mark your answer.

A   Multiply the number of minutes by the number of newspapers

B   Multiply the number of newspapers by 5

C   Divide the number of newspapers by the number of minutes

D   Add the number of newspapers and number of minutes

Reporting Category 2 – 4.5 (B) Algebraic Reasoning

☐ Alyssa kept a record of the number of red birds and robins she saw in one week. She recorded her findings 3 times a day. The chart below shows her results. From these results, which statement would most likely be true? Mark your answer.

Red Birds	Robins
ⅢⅠ II	ⅢⅠ IIII

Each tally is equal to 4 birds.

A   There were more red birds than robins.

B   There were fewer red birds than robins.

C   There were twice as many robins as red birds.

D   She saw the same number of both kinds of birds.

Reporting Category 2 – 4.5 (B) Algebraic Reasoning

☐   The table below shows the amount of money Dylan has saved over several months.

Number of Months	Amount Saved
3	$15
7	$35
5	$25
11	$55

What is one way to find the amount of money he will save in one year? Mark your answer.

A   Divide the amount saved by the number of months

B   Subtract the number of months from the amount saved

C   Add the total number of months to the total amount saved

D   Multiply 12 × 5

Reporting Category 2 – 4.5 (B) Algebraic Reasoning

☐   The table shows the sales of some school supplies at Butler Intermediate. Based on the information below, which statement would most likely be true? Mark your answer.

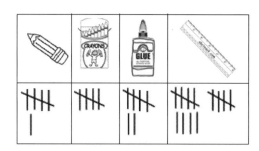

A   The 4 items had an equal number of sales.

B   There were twice as many rulers sold as bottles of glue.

C   There were less pencils sold than boxes of crayons.

D   The total sales of all 4 items is 31.

Reporting Category 2 – 4.5 (B) Algebraic Reasoning

☐ The table below shows the number of boxes of cookies Mrs. Clements must buy for the refreshments for a club meeting.

Number of Boxes	Number of Cookies
3	36
5	
6	72
10	120

What is one way to find the number of cookies Mrs. Clemmer will buy if she buys 5 boxes? Mark your answer.

A   Divide the number of cookies into the number of boxes

B   Add 5 to 36

C   Multiply 5 by 12

D   Subtract 5 from 36

Reporting Category 2 – 4.5 (B) Algebraic Reasoning

☐ The table below shows the number of gallons of ice cream needed to serve students who eat lunch each day in the school cafeteria. Mark your answer.

Number of Students	Number of Gallons
84	7
108	9
144	12

A   Number of students ÷ 7 = number of gallons

B   Number of students × 7 = number of gallons

C   Number of students × 12 = number of gallons

D   Number of students ÷ 12 = number of gallons

Reporting Category 2 – 4.5 (B) Algebraic Reasoning

☐ The table below shows results of an experiment students conducted using a rubber band to propel a toy car across a bridge. They used a stopwatch to measure the time it took the car to cross the bridge.

Number of times toy car crossed the bridge	Number of seconds for toy car to cross the bridge
1	1.5
4	6
5	7.5
3	4.5
8	12

Which of the following correctly describes the relationship in the table? Mark your answer.

A   Number of seconds × 1.5 = number of times

B   Number of seconds ÷ 1 = number of times

C   Number of seconds ÷ 1.5 = number of times

D   Number of seconds × 1 = number of times

Reporting Category 2 – 4.5 (B) Algebraic Reasoning

☐ Logan conducted a survey to find the favorite TV channel of 10 families in his neighborhood. The table shows the results of the survey. From these results, which statement would most likely be true? Mark your answer.

Favorite TV Channels

Channel 2	Channel 7	Channel 10
3	2	5

A   Half as many people chose Channel 2 as those who chose Channel 10

B   Twice as many people chose Channel 10 as those who chose Channel 3

C   Fewer people chose Channel 7 than those who chose Channel 2

D   Less people chose Channel 2 than those who chose Channel 7

Name _____

Reporting Category 2 – 4.5 (B) Algebraic Reasoning

☐ **The table shows the regular prices of movie tickets and the discounted prices on certain days.**

Day	Regular Price	Discounted Price
Thursday	$3.75	$2.75
Friday	$5.75	$4.75
Saturday	$5.75	$4.75
Sunday	$4.75	$3.75

Based on the information in the table, which could be the discount offered? Mark your answer.

A   Take $2.75 off the regular price

B   Take $1.75 off the regular price

C   Go to the movie on Thursday night

D   Take $1 off the regular price

Reporting Category 2 – 4.5 (B) Algebraic Reasoning

☐ **Each number in Set X is paired with a number in Set Z.**

Set X	Set Z
27	9
33	11
12	4
24	8

Which of the following correctly describes the relationship in the table? Mark your answer.

A   Set Z ÷ 3 = Set X

B   Set Z + 27 = Set X

C   Set Z ÷ 9 = Set X

D   Set Z × 3 = Set X

Reporting Category 2 – 4.5 (B) Algebraic Reasoning

☐ Each number in Set A is paired with a number in Set B.

Set A	Set B
3	18
6	
4	24
12	72

What is one way to find the missing number in Set B? Mark your answer.

A   Divide 6 by 3

B   Divide 18 by 6

C   Add 3, 6, 4, 12, and 18

D   Multiply 6 by 6

Reporting Category 2 – 4.5 (B) Algebraic Reasoning

☐ Each number in Set M is related in the same way to the number beside it in Set P.

Set M	Set P
4	32
2	16
6	48
40	320

When given a number in Set M, what is one way to find its related number in Set P? Mark your answer.

A   Divide by 8

B   Multiply by 8

C   Add 28

D   Subtract 4

Name _____

Reporting Category 2 – 4.5 (B) Algebraic Reasoning

☐ **Mrs. Bolton made a table to show how she increased the amount of eggs in a recipe to make more than one dozen cookies.**

Number of Dozen	Number of Eggs
4	12
6	18
7	21
9	27

What is one way to find the number of eggs she will use if she makes 2 dozen cookies? Mark your answer.

A Multiply the number of eggs by 3

B Multiply the number of eggs by the number of dozen

C Multiply the number of dozens of cookies by 3

D Divide the number of eggs by the number of dozen

Reporting Category 2 – 4.5 (B) Algebraic Reasoning

☐ **Humberto made a table of the heights of some of his friends.**

Name	Height (in.)
Wyatt	47
Lucas	41
Bryan	49
Jackson	44

Based on the information in the table, which statement would most likely be true? Mark your answer.

A There is a 2 inch difference in each boys' height.

B None of the boys are as tall as Wyatt.

C Bryan is the only boy who is over 4 feet tall.

D Jackson is 3 inches shorter than Lucas.

Reporting Category 3 – 4.5 (D) Algebraic Reasoning

☐ **Mr. Thomas bought fencing for his yard. About how many meters of fencing should he buy to enclose the entire yard? Mark your answer.**

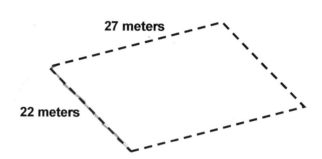

A   60 meters

B   160 meters

C   100 meters

D   50 meters

27 meters

22 meters

Reporting Category 3 – 4.5 (D) Algebraic Reasoning

☐ **A builder wants to cover a wall with brick. The wall measures 56 meters long and 8 meters wide. About how large is the area to be covered with brick? Mark your answer.**

A   70 square meters

B   140 square meters

C   60 square meters

D   600 square meters

Reporting Category 3 – 4.5 (D) Algebraic Reasoning

☐ **A city built a new swimming pool at a park. The length of the pool is 48 feet and the width is 27 feet. If a pad is added to the edges of the pool to prevent injuries, about how many feet of padding is needed? Mark your answer.**

A   140 feet

B   160 feet

C   80 feet

D   75 feet

Reporting Category 3 – 4.5 (D) Algebraic Reasoning

☐ Cameron bought a piece of drawing board. If the drawing board costs 2¢ per square inch, about how many square inches did the clerk use to calculate the cost of the product? Mark your answer.

A   45 square inches

B   60 square inches

C   120 square inches

D   900 square inches

25 inches

34 inches

Reporting Category 3 – 4.5 (D) Algebraic Reasoning

☐ Ms. Bacon bought lace to put around the edges of a pillow. About how much lace did Ms. Bacon buy? Mark your answer.

14 centimeters

A   28   centimeters

B   60   centimeters

C   80   centimeters

D   20 centimeters

Reporting Category 3 – 4.5 (D) Algebraic Reasoning

☐ A large lake measures 12 kilometers long and 4 kilometers wide. About how many square kilometers does the lake cover? Mark your answer.

A   16 square kilometers

B   32 square kilometers

C   40 square kilometers

D   100 square kilometers

Reporting Category 3 – 4.5 (D) Algebraic Reasoning

☐ **Ms. Arnold put border around a bulletin board in her classroom. About how much border did she use? Mark your answer.**

A   200 inches

B   160 inches

C   150 inches

D   100 inches

45 inches

Reporting Category 3 – 4.5 (D) Algebraic Reasoning

☐ **A carpet company is replacing the carpet in a library. The floor to be covered measures 71 feet by 47 feet. About how many square feet of new carpeting will be used? Mark your answer.**

A   120 square feet

B   350 square feet

C   2800 square feet

D   3500 square feet

Reporting Category 3 – 4.5 (D) Algebraic Reasoning

☐ **A card measured 15 millimeters by 22 millimeters. Estimate the perimeter of the card. Mark your answer.**

A   37 millimeters

B   60 millimeters

C   40 millimeters

D   80 millimeters

Reporting Category 3 – 4.5 (D) Algebraic Reasoning

☐ Estimate the area of the shape below. Mark your answer.

A   400 sq cm

B   600 sq cm

C   40 sq cm

D   80 sq cm

36 centimeters

11 centimeters

Reporting Category 3 – 4.5 (D) Algebraic Reasoning

☐ A piece of fabric was 81 yards long and 3 yards wide. Estimate the perimeter of the piece of fabric. Mark your answer.

A   84 yards

B   240 yards

C   166 yards

D   83 yards

Reporting Category 3 – 4.5 (D) Algebraic Reasoning

☐ About how many square yards of roofing tiles are needed to cover an area that measures 19 yards by 5 yards? Mark your answer.

A   100 square yards

B   200 square yards

C   50 square yards

D   60 square yards

Reporting Category 3 – 4.6 (A) Geometry and Measurement

☐   **Renee's mother baked an apple pie. She cut the pie into 8 parts. Which two lines form perpendicular lines when they cross? Mark your answer.**

A   (A and B)

B   (A and D)

C   (A and C)

D   (B and C)

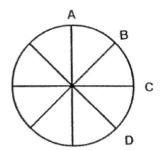

Reporting Category 3 – 4.6 (A) Geometry and Measurement

☐   **Look at the sets of lines. Which shows a set of parallel lines? Mark your answer.**

A   D

B   B

C   C

D   A

Reporting Category 3 – 4.6 (A) Geometry and Measurement

☐   **Look at the compass rose. Identify the type of lines the primary direction lines form. Mark your answer.**

A   Perpendicular

B   Parallel

C   Acute

D   Curved

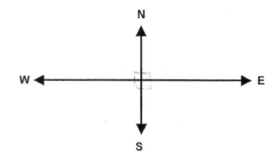

Reporting Category 3 – 4.6 (A) Geometry and Measurement

☐ **Which term describes the lines on the US Flag below? Mark your answer.**

A   **Acute**

B   **Intersecting**

C   **Parallel**

D   **Perpendicular**

Reporting Category 3 – 4.6 (A) Geometry and Measurement

☐ **Look at the lines below, which answer best describes the lines? Mark your answer.**

A   **Perpendicular**

B   **Parallel**

C   **Congruent**

D   **Intersecting**

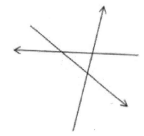

Reporting Category 3 – 4.6 (A) Geometry and Measurement

☐ **Which of the following statements is true? Mark your answer.**

A   **Parallel lines intersect only once.**

B   **Parallel lines always include perpendicular lines.**

C   **Parallel lines are always the same length.**

D   **Parallel lines never intersect.**

Reporting Category 3 – 4.6 (A) Geometry and Measurement

☐ **Which drawing best represents a figure with only one pair of parallel lines? Mark your answer.**

A

Ç

B

D

Reporting Category 3 – 4.6 (A) Geometry and Measurement

☐ **Which statement is true about a rhombus?   Mark your answer.**

A   It has two pairs of parallel sides and two pairs of equal angles.

B   It has only two pairs of parallel sides and two pairs of equal sides.

C   It has only two pairs of equal angles.

D   It has only two pairs of equal sides.

Reporting Category 3 – 4.6 (A) Geometry and Measurement

☐ **Which statement is true about the line segments in the square below? Mark your answer.**

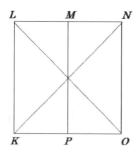

A   Line segments *KO* and *MP* are parallel.

B   Line segments *LO* and *KN* are parallel.

C   Line segments *MP* and *LN* are perpendicular.

D   Line segments *KL* and *KN* are perpendicular.

Reporting Category 3 – 4.6 (A) Geometry and Measurement

☐ **Which shapes below have only two parallel sides? Mark your answer.**

A   Rhombus

B   Trapezoid

C   Parallelogram

D   Pentagon

Reporting Category 3 – 4.6 (A) Geometry and Measurement

☐ **Which drawing best represents a figure with more than one pair of parallel lines? Mark your answer.**

A   C

B   D

Reporting Category 3 – 4.6 (A) Geometry and Measurement

☐ **Which statement about the line segments in this triangle is not true? Mark your answer.**

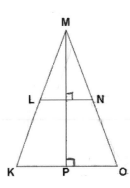

A   Line segments *LN* and *KO* are parallel.

B   Line segments *KO* and *MP* are perpendicular.

C   Line segments *LN* and *MP* are perpendicular.

D   Line segments *KL* and *NO* are perpendicular.

Reporting Category 3 – 4.6 (B) Geometry and Measurement

☐ **Which of these drawings has exactly 1 line of symmetry? Mark your answer.**

A

B

C

D

Reporting Category 3 – 4.6 (B) Geometry and Measurement

☐ **Which number has at least one line of symmetry? Mark your answer.**

A **6**   C **3**

B **5**   D **4**

Reporting Category 3 – 4.6 (B) Geometry and Measurement

☐ **Which statement is true about the letters shown below? Mark your answer.**

M Y I B E

A   None of the letters have a line of symmetry.

B   They all have more than one line of symmetry.

C   They have exactly one line of symmetry.

D   They have at least one line of symmetry.

Reporting Category 3 – 4.6 (B) Geometry and Measurement

☐ **Which does not show a line of symmetry? Mark your answer.**

A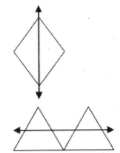

B

C

D

Reporting Category 3 – 4.6 (B) Geometry and Measurement

☐ **Which letter has at least one line of symmetry? Mark your answer.**

A **B**

B **H**

C **V**

D **C**

Reporting Category 3 – 4.6 (B) Geometry and Measurement

☐ **Which figure shows a line of symmetry? Mark your answer.**

A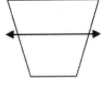

B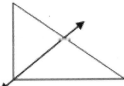

C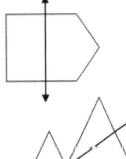

D

Reporting Category 3 – 4.6 (B) Geometry and Measurement

☐ **Which statement is not true about the numbers shown below? Mark your answer.**

9 4 2 7

A   They all have at least one line of symmetry.

B   None of the numbers have one line of symmetry.

C   None of the numbers have more than one line of symmetry.

D   None of the numbers have exactly one line of symmetry.

Reporting Category 3 – 4.6 (B) Geometry and Measurement

☐ **Which letter has a line of symmetry? Mark your answer.**

A   **J**   C   **P**

B   **Q**   D   **T**

Reporting Category 3 – 4.6 (B) Geometry and Measurement

☐ **Which figure does not have a line of symmetry? Mark your answer.**

A   C

B      D

Reporting Category 3 – 4.6 (B) Geometry and Measurement

☐ **Which figure shows a line of symmetry? Mark your answer.**

A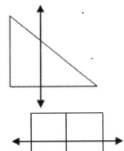

C

B

D

Reporting Category 3 – 4.6 (B) Geometry and Measurement

☐ **Which letter does not have a line of symmetry? Mark your answer.**

A **D**

C **E**

B **G**

D **Y**

Reporting Category 3 – 4.6 (B) Geometry and Measurement

☐ **Which figure has more than one line of symmetry? Mark your answer.**

A

C

B

D

Reporting Category 3 – 4.6 (B) Geometry and Measurement

Which does not show a figure with a line of symmetry? Mark your answer.

A

C

B

D

Reporting Category 3 – 4.6 (B) Geometry and Measurement

Which letter has only one line of symmetry? Mark your answer.

A

C

B

D

Reporting Category 3 – 4.6 (B) Geometry and Measurement

Which number has two lines of symmetry? Mark your answer.

A **9**

C **8**

B **3**

D **4**

Name _____

Reporting Category 3 – 4.6 (B) Geometry and Measurement

☐ **Which figure shows a line of symmetry? Mark your answer.**

A

C

B

D

Reporting Category 3 – 4.6 (B) Geometry and Measurement

☐ **Which statement is true about the numbers shown? Mark your answer.**

2 5 9 6

A   They have more than one line of symmetry.

B   They do not have any lines of symmetry.

C   They all have exactly two lines of symmetry.

D   They have at least one line of symmetry.

Reporting Category 3 – 4.6 (B) Geometry and Measurement

☐ **Which number has only one line of symmetry? Mark your answer.**

A **4**

C

B **8**

D **0**

Reporting Category 3 – 4.6 (B) Geometry and Measurement

☐ **Which statement is not true about the numbers and letters shown? Mark your answer.**

A   They have more than one line of symmetry.

B   They do not have any lines of symmetry.

C   They all have exactly two lines of symmetry.

D   They have at least one line of symmetry.

Reporting Category 3 – 4.6 (B) Geometry and Measurement

☐ **Which figure has a line of symmetry? Mark your answer.**

 A

 **C**

 B

 **D**

Reporting Category 3 – 4.6 (B) Geometry and Measurement

☐ **Which does not show a line of symmetry? Mark your answer.**

A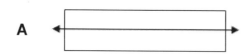

C

B

D

Name _____

Reporting Category 3 – 4.6 (B) Geometry and Measurement

☐ **Which number has only one line of symmetry? Mark your answer.**

A **0**

B **5**

C **3**

D **8**

Reporting Category 3 – 4.6 (B) Geometry and Measurement

☐ **Which figure shows a line of symmetry? Mark your answer.**

A

B

C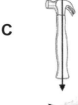

D

Reporting Category 3 – 4.6 (B) Geometry and Measurement

☐ **Which numbers and letters have two lines of symmetry? Mark your answer.**

3 8 Y 0 E

A   8 and Y

B   0 and 8

C   E and 3

D   0 and E

© **Teachers' Treasures Publishing**

Reporting Category 3 – 4.6 (C) Geometry and Measurement

☐ **Angle *M* in the figure below appears to be which kind of angle? Mark your answer.**

A   **Right**

B   **Straight**

C   **Obtuse**

D   **Acute**

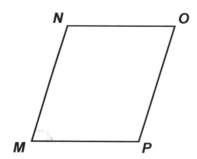

Reporting Category 3 – 4.6 (C) Geometry and Measurement

☐ **What angle is formed when perpendicular lines meet? Mark your answer.**

A   **Obtuse**

B   **Acute**

C   **Right**

D   **Strai**

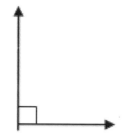

Reporting Category 3 – 4.6 (C) Geometry and Measurement

☐ **What kind of angle does ∠*B* appear to be in the hexagon? Mark your answer.**

A   **Acute**

B   **Obtuse**

C   **Straight**

D   **Right**

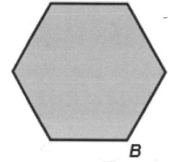

Reporting Category 3 – 4.6 (C) Geometry and Measurement

☐ Based on the drawing of the desk, which of the following does the top of the desk appear to be made up of? Mark your answer.

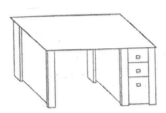

A Right and obtuse angles

B Right and acute angles

C Right angles only

D Acute and obtuse angles

Reporting Category 3 – 4.6 (C) Geometry and Measurement

☐ Which of the following is the greatest angle? Mark your answer.

A

B

C

D

Reporting Category 3 – 4.6 (C) Geometry and Measurement

☐ **What kind of angle is formed beneath the telescope? Mark your answer.**

A   Obtuse

B   Right

C   Acute

D   Straight

Reporting Category 3 – 4.6 (C) Geometry and Measurement

☐ **When Highway 151 and Interstate 10 meet, what kind of angle is formed? Mark your answer.**

A   Straight

B   Obtuse

C   Acute

D   Right

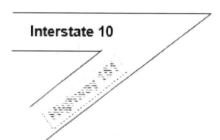

Interstate 10

Reporting Category 3 – 4.6 (C) Geometry and Measurement

☐ **Which of the following is the least angle? Mark your answer.**

A

B

C

D

Name _____

PRACTICE

Reporting Category 3 – 4.6 (C) Geometry and Measurement

☐ **Which pair of angles could be put together to form a right angle? Mark your answer.**

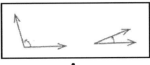

A

B

C

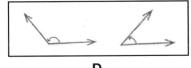

D

A   B

B   D

C   A

D   C

Reporting Category 3 – 4.6 (C) Geometry and Measurement

☐ **The shelf is made up of 6 sections. Which of the following is an angle found in one of the sections of the shelf? Mark your answer.**

A   Obtuse angle only

B   Right angle only

C   Right and obtuse angles

D   Acute angle only

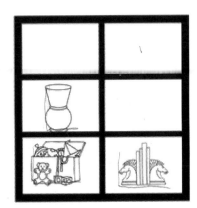

Reporting Category 3 – 4.6 (C) Geometry and Measurement

Which of the angles represents an obtuse angle?   Mark your answer.

A   Angle C

B   Angle B

C   Angle A

D   Angle D

Reporting Category 3 – 4.6 (C) Geometry and Measurement

What kind of angle is formed by the legs on the inside of the letter "W"?
Mark your answer.

A   Obtuse

B   Right

C   Straight

D   Acute

Reporting Category 3 – 4.6 (C) Geometry and Measurement

Which best describes the angle formed by the lawn chair? Mark your
answer.

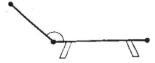

A   Acute

B   Right

C   Obtuse

D   Straight

Reporting Category 3 – 4.6 (C) Geometry and Measurement

☐ **Which clock's hands form an obtuse angle? Mark your answer.**

A    C

B    D

Reporting Category 3 – 4.6 (C) Geometry and Measurement

☐ **Which angle is greater than a right angle? Mark your answer.**

A

B

C

D

Reporting Category 3 – 4.6 (C) Geometry and Measurement

☐ **Which correctly describes the angle shown on the protractor? Mark your answer.**

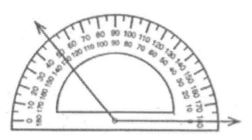

A   Acute angle of 50°

B   Obtuse angle of 50°

C   Obtuse angle of 130°

D   Acute angle of 130°

Reporting Category 3 – 4.6 (C) Geometry and Measurement

☐ **Which angle is less than a straight angle, but greater than a right angle? Mark your answer.**

A      C

B   D 

Reporting Category 3 – 4.6 (C) Geometry and Measurement

☐ **Which two angles could be put together to form an acute angle? Mark your answer.**

A   Angle C and D

B   Angle B and C

C   Angle A and C

D   Angle B and D

Reporting Category 3 – 4.6 (C) Geometry and Measurement

☐ **What angle do the clock's hands form? Mark your answer.**

A   Right

B   Acute

C   Obtuse

D   Straight

Reporting Category 3 – 4.6 (C) Geometry and Measurement

☐ **Which angle in the drawing below is a right angle? Mark your answer.**

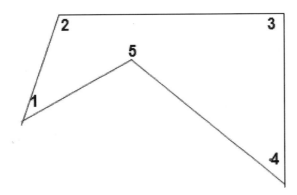

A   5

B   1

C   3

D   2

Reporting Category 3 – 4.6 (D) Geometry and Measurement

☐ Isaac placed four straws on a table. Which two straws appear to be perpendicular to each other? Mark your answer.

A   Straws 1 and 3

B   Straws 2 and 4

C   Straws 2 and 3

D   Straws 1 and 2

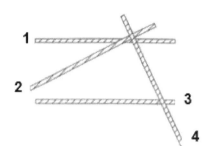

Reporting Category 3 – 4.6 (D) Geometry and Measurement

☐ Which line is parallel to $\overleftrightarrow{LN}$? Mark your answer.

A $\overleftrightarrow{LM}$

B $\overleftrightarrow{MQ}$

C $\overleftrightarrow{MR}$

D $\overleftrightarrow{PR}$

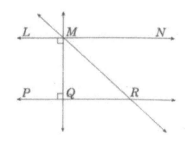

Reporting Category 3 – 4.6 (D) Geometry and Measurement

☐ In the rectangle below, which statement about the line segments is true? Mark your answer.

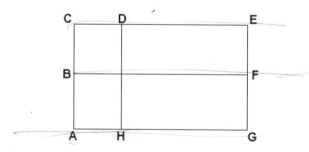

A   Line segments *BF* and *AC* are parallel.

B   Line segments *CD* and *HA* are parallel.

C   Line segments *GA* and *CE* are perpendicular.

D   Line segments *BF* and *CE* are perpendicular.

Reporting Category 3 – 4.6 (D) Geometry and Measurement

Which of the following best describes the legs of the table in relation to each other? Mark your answer.

A   Wavy lines

B   Parallel lines

C   Perpendicular lines

D   Curved lines

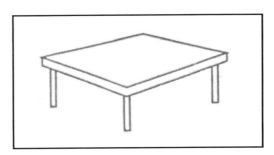

Reporting Category 3 – 4.6 (D) Geometry and Measurement

Which two streets are parallel in the map below? Mark your answer.

A   Center Avenue and Broad Boulevard

B   Alley Street and Broad Boulevard

C   Bonner Street and Alley Street

D   Bonner Street and Center Avenue

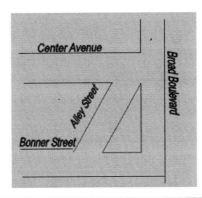

Reporting Category 3 – 4.6 (D) Geometry and Measurement

Which drawing best represents a figure with only one pair of parallel lines? Mark your answer.

A

C

B

D

Reporting Category 3 – 4.6 (D) Geometry and Measurement

☐   **Which statement about the line segments in this triangle is not true? Mark your answer.**

A   Wavy

B   Parallel

C   Diagonal

D   Curved

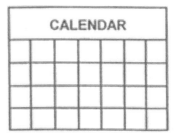

Reporting Category 3 – 4.6 (D) Geometry and Measurement

☐   **Which term describes the two streets? Mark your answer.**

A   Acute

B   Horizontal

C   Parallel

D   Perpendicular

Reporting Category 3 – 4.6 (D) Geometry and Measurement

☐   **Which statement about the line segments in this rectangle is not true? Mark your answer.**

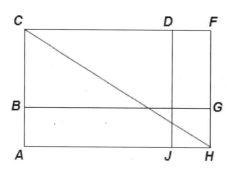

A   Line segments *DJ* and *BG* are perpendicular.

B   Line segments *AH* and *CF* are perpendicular.

C   Line segments *AC* and *DJ* are parallel.

D   Line segments *FH* and *DJ* are parallel.

Reporting Category 3 – 4.6 (D) Geometry and Measurement

☐ **Which streets are perpendicular? Mark your answer.**

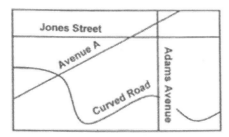

A   Jones Street and Avenue A

B   Jones Street and Adams Avenue

C   None of the streets

D   Curved Road and Jones Street

Reporting Category 3 – 4.6 (D) Geometry and Measurement

☐ **Which drawing has 2 line segments that appear to be parallel? Mark your answer.**

A

C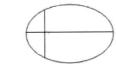

B

D

Reporting Category 3 – 4.6 (D) Geometry and Measurement

☐ **Which drawing best represents a figure with more than two pair of parallel lines? Mark your answer.**

A

C

B

D

Reporting Category 3 – 4.7 (C) Geometry and Measurement

Look at the protractor below. What is the angle measurement for lines *DAF*? Mark your answer.

A   105º

B   180º

C   75º

D   90º

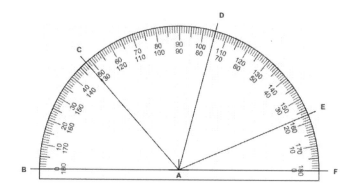

Reporting Category 3 – 4.7 (C) Geometry and Measurement

Look at the protractor below. What is the angle measurement for lines *CAB*? Mark your answer.

A   48º

B   130º

C   180º

D   105º

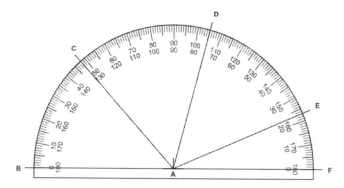

Reporting Category 3 – 4.7 (C) Geometry and Measurement

Look at the protractor below. What is the angle measurement for lines *EAF*? Mark your answer.

A   157º

B   180º

C   35º

D   23º

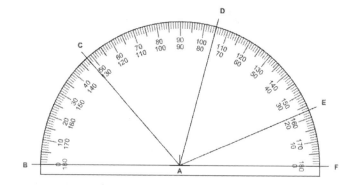

Reporting Category 3 – 4.7 (C) Geometry and Measurement

☐ **Look at the protractor below. What is the angle measurement for lines *DAB*? Mark your answer.**

A   70º

B   109º

C   169º

D   180º

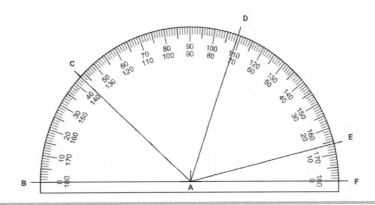

Reporting Category 3 – 4.7 (C) Geometry and Measurement

☐ **Look at the protractor below. What is the angle measurement for lines *DAF*? Mark your answer.**

A   43º

B   109º

C   80º

D   71º

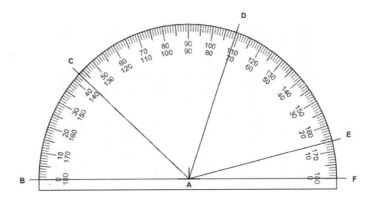

Reporting Category 3 – 4.7 (C) Geometry and Measurement

☐ **Look at the protractor below. What is the angle measurement for lines *EAB*? Mark your answer.**

A   14º

B   170º

C   166º

D   180º

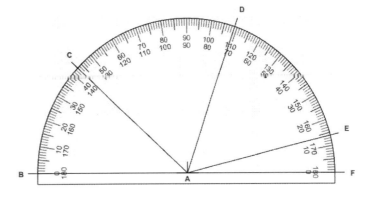

Name _____

☐　　**Look at the protractor below. What is the angle measurement for lines *EAB*? Mark your answer.**

A　　157º

B　　165º

C　　23º

D　　180º

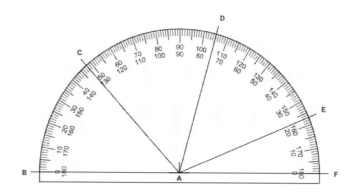

☐　　**Look at the protractor below. What is the angle measurement for lines *CAF*? Mark your answer.**

A　　48º

B　　132º

C　　140º

D　　180º

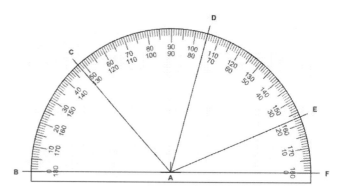

☐　　**Look at the protractor below. What is the angle measurement for lines *DAB*? Mark your answer.**

A　　75º

B　　110º

C　　105º

D　　90º

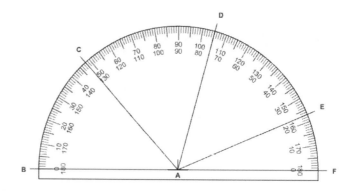

Reporting Category 3 – 4.7 (C) Geometry and Measurement

☐ **Look at the protractor below. What is the angle measurement for lines *CAF*? Mark your answer.**

A   **137°**

B   **43°**

C   **183°**

D   **166°**

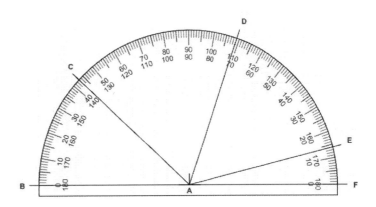

Reporting Category 3 – 4.7 (C) Geometry and Measurement

☐ **Look at the protractor below. What is the angle measurement for lines *DAF*? Mark your answer.**

A   **175°**

B   **90°**

C   **81°**

D   **99°**

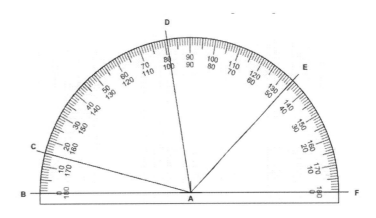

Reporting Category 3 – 4.7 (C) Geometry and Measurement

☐ **Look at the protractor below. What is the angle measurement for lines *EAB*? Mark your answer.**

A   **180°**

B   **56°**

C   **134°**

D   **0°**

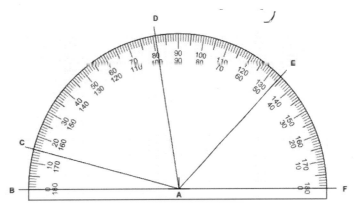

Reporting Category 3 – 4.7 (C) Geometry and Measurement

☐ Look at the protractor below. What is the angle measurement for lines *CAB*? Mark your answer.

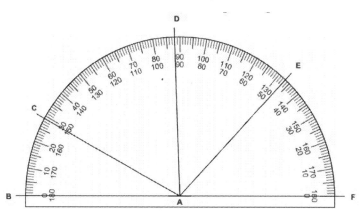

A   151º

B   160º

C   29º

D   88º

Reporting Category 3 – 4.7 (C) Geometry and Measurement

☐ Look at the protractor below. What is the angle measurement for lines *DAF*? Mark your answer.

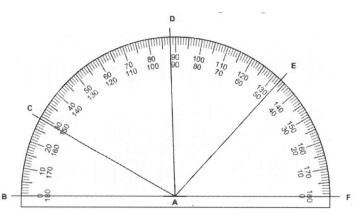

A   92º

B   90º

C   80º

D   180º

Reporting Category 3 – 4.7 (C) Geometry and Measurement

☐ Look at the protractor below. What is the angle measurement for lines *EAB*? Mark your answer.

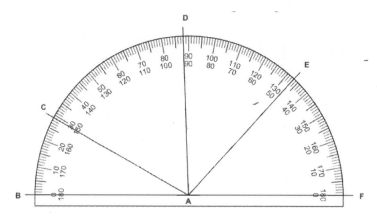

A   55º

B   133º

C   135º

D   53º

Name _____

Reporting Category 3 – 4.7 (C) Geometry and Measurement

☐ Look at the protractor below. What is the angle measurement for lines *DAB*? Mark your answer.

A   78°

B   80°

C   103°

D   100°

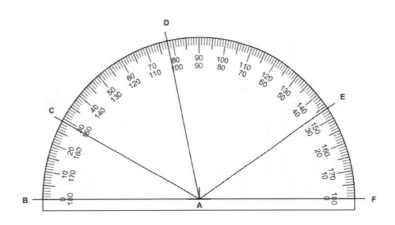

Reporting Category 3 – 4.7 (C) Geometry and Measurement

☐ Look at the protractor below. What is the angle measurement for Lines *CAF?* Mark your answer.

A   150°

B   30°

C   151°

D   180°

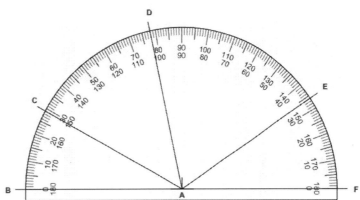

Reporting Category 3 – 4.7 (C) Geometry and Measurement

☐ Look at the protractor below. What is the angle measurement for lines *EAF?* Mark your answer.

A   147°

B   34°

C   33°

D   150°

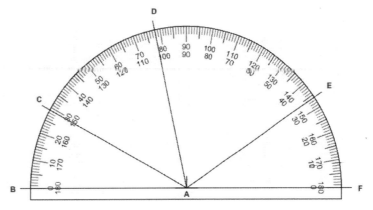

Reporting Category 3 – 4.7 (C) Geometry and Measurement

Look at the protractor below. What is the angle measurement for lines *CAB*? Mark your answer.

A   180°

B   155°

C   35°

D   25°

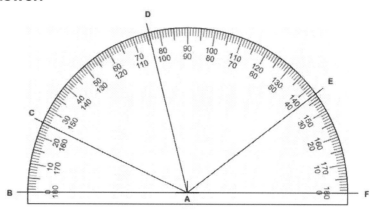

Reporting Category 3 – 4.7 (C) Geometry and Measurement

Look at the protractor below. What is the angle measurement for lines *CAF*? Mark your answer.

A   25°

B   155°

C   35°

D   165°

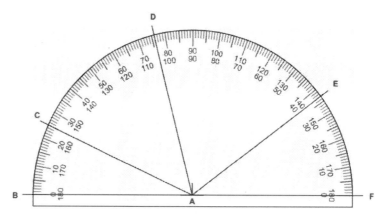

Reporting Category 3 – 4.7 (C) Geometry and Measurement

Look at the protractor below. What is the angle measurement for lines *DAF*? Mark your answer.

A   76°

B   116°

C   104°

D   84°

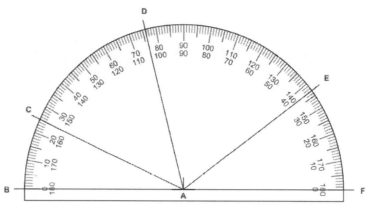

Reporting Category 3 – 4.7 (C) Geometry and Measurement

☐ Look at the protractor below. What is the angle measurement for lines *DAB*? Mark your answer.

A 113º

B 70º

C 115º

D 67º

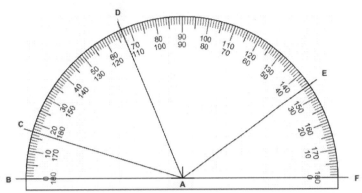

Reporting Category 3 – 4.7 (C) Geometry and Measurement

☐ Look at the protractor below. What is the angle measurement for lines *CAF*? Mark your answer.

A 17º

B 18º

C 163º

D 180º

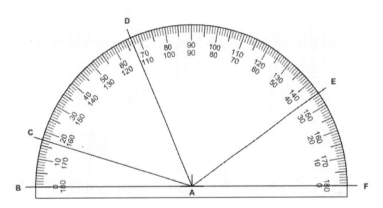

Reporting Category 3 – 4.7 (C) Geometry and Measurement

☐ Look at the protractor below. What is the angle measurement for lines *DAF*? Mark your answer.

A 113º

B 67º

C 72º

D 145º

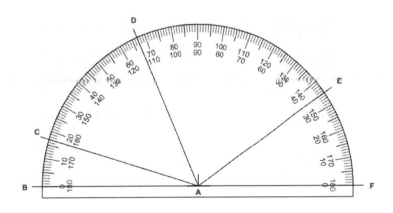

Reporting Category 3 – 4.7 (D) Geometry and Measurement

☐ **Use your protractor to draw an angle measurement that is 70º.**

_____

Reporting Category 3 – 4.7 (D) Geometry and Measurement

☐ **Use your protractor to draw an angle measurement that is 18º.**

_____

Reporting Category 3 – 4.7 (D) Geometry and Measurement

☐ **Use your protractor to draw an angle measurement that is 145º.**

_____

Reporting Category 3 – 4.7 (D) Geometry and Measurement

☐ **Use your protractor to draw an angle measurement that is 169º.**

_____

Reporting Category 3 – 4.7 (D) Geometry and Measurement

☐ **Use your protractor to draw an angle measurement that is 90º.**

_____

Reporting Category 3 – 4.7 (D) Geometry and Measurement

☐ **Use your protractor to draw an angle measurement that is 23º.**

_____

Reporting Category 3 – 4.7 (D) Geometry and Measurement

☐ **Use your protractor to draw an angle measurement that is 14º.**

_____

Reporting Category 3 – 4.7 (D) Geometry and Measurement

☐ **Use your protractor to draw an angle measurement that is 180º.**

_____

Reporting Category 3 – 4.7 (D) Geometry and Measurement

☐ **Use your protractor to draw an angle measurement that is 75º.**

_____

Reporting Category 3 – 4.7 (D) Geometry and Measurement

☐   **Use your protractor to draw an angle measurement that is 117°.**

_____

Reporting Category 3 – 4.7 (D) Geometry and Measurement

☐   **Use your protractor to draw an angle measurement that is 56°.**

_____

Reporting Category 3 – 4.7 (D) Geometry and Measurement

☐   **Use your protractor to draw an angle measurement that is 29°.**

_____

Reporting Category 3 – 4.7 (D) Geometry and Measurement

☐   **Use your protractor to draw an angle measurement that is 167°.**

_____

Reporting Category 3 – 4.7 (D) Geometry and Measurement

☐   **Use your protractor to draw an angle measurement that is 90°.**

_____

Reporting Category 3 – 4.7 (D) Geometry and Measurement

☐   **Use your protractor to draw an angle measurement that is 172°.**

_____

Reporting Category 3 – 4.7 (D) Geometry and Measurement

☐ **Use your protractor to draw an angle measurement that is 38º.**

_____

Reporting Category 3 – 4.7 (D) Geometry and Measurement

☐ **Use your protractor to draw an angle measurement that is 77º.**

_____

Reporting Category 3 – 4.7 (D) Geometry and Measurement

☐ **Use your protractor to draw an angle measurement that is 179º.**

_____

Reporting Category 3 – 4.7 (D) Geometry and Measurement

☐ **Use your protractor to draw an angle measurement that is 31º.**

_____

Reporting Category 3 – 4.7 (D) Geometry and Measurement

☐ **Use your protractor to draw an angle measurement that is 111º.**

_____

Reporting Category 3 – 4.7 (D) Geometry and Measurement

☐ **Use your protractor to draw an angle measurement that is 61º.**

_____

Name _____

Reporting Category 3 – 4.7 (D) Geometry and Measurement

☐   **Use your protractor to draw an angle measurement that is 94°.**

Reporting Category 3 – 4.7 (D) Geometry and Measurement

☐   **Use your protractor to draw an angle measurement that is 100°.**

Reporting Category 3 – 4.7 (D) Geometry and Measurement

☐   **Use your protractor to draw an angle measurement that is 44°.**

Reporting Category 3 – 4.7 (E) Geometry and Measurement

Find the measurement for ∠ABD if ∠ABC = 55° and ∠CBD= 25°. Mark your answer.

A   30º

B   80º

C   90º

D   55º

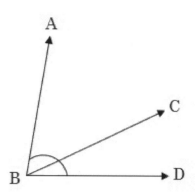

Reporting Category 3 – 4.7 (E) Geometry and Measurement

Find the measurement for ∠ GFH if ∠ EFH = 120° and ∠ EFG = 30°. Mark your answer.

A   80º

B   150º

C   90º

D   30º

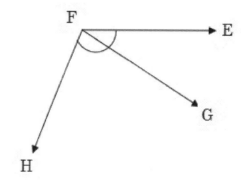

Reporting Category 3 – 4.7 (E) Geometry and Measurement

Find the measurement for ∠ IJL if ∠ IJK = 80° and ∠ KJL = 60°. Mark your answer.

A   130º

B   20º

C   80º

D   140º

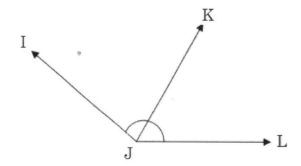

Reporting Category 3 – 4.7 (E) Geometry and Measurement

☐ **Find the measurement for ∠ CBD if ∠ ABD = 130° and ∠ ABC= 90°. Mark your answer.**

A   30°

B   240°

C   40°

D   90°

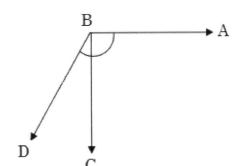

Reporting Category 3 – 4.7 (E) Geometry and Measurement

☐ **Find the measurement for ∠ EFH if ∠ GFH = 25° and ∠ EFG = 45°. Mark your answer.**

A   70°

B   20°

C   80°

D   45°

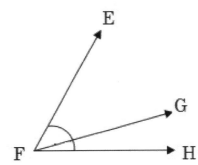

Reporting Category 3 – 4.7 (E) Geometry and Measurement

☐ **Find the measurement for ∠ KJL if ∠ IJL = 130° and ∠ IJK = 100°. Mark your answer.**

A   230°

B   40°

C   100°

D   30°

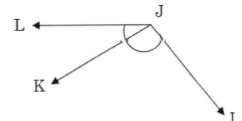

Reporting Category 3 – 4.7 (E) Geometry and Measurement

☐ Find the measurement for ∠ ABD if ∠ ABC = 15° and ∠ CBD= 45°. Mark your answer.

A   60°

B   80°

C   30°

D   45°

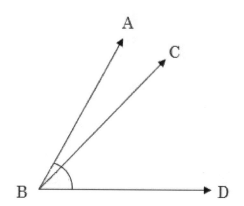

Reporting Category 3 – 4.7 (E) Geometry and Measurement

☐ Find the measurement for ∠ GFH if ∠ EFH = 150° and ∠ EFG = 75°. Mark your answer.

A   110°

B   150°

C   75°

D   80°

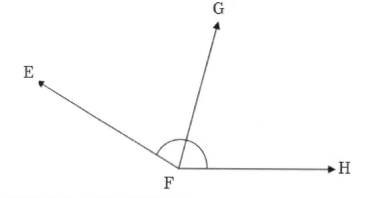

Reporting Category 3 – 4.7 (E) Geometry and Measurement

☐ Find the measurement for ∠ IJL if ∠ IJK = 70° and ∠ KJL = 40°. Mark your answer.

A   30°

B   112°

C   70°

D   110°

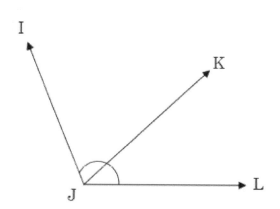

Reporting Category 3 – 4.7 (E) Geometry and Measurement

☐ **Find the measurement for ∠ ABC if ∠ ABD = 80° and ∠ CBD= 40°. Mark your answer.**

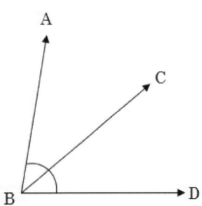

A   80°

B   120°

C   40°

D   45°

Common Core Standard 4.MD.7 – Measurement & Data

☐ **Find the measurement for ∠ EFH if ∠ GFH = 55° and ∠ EFG = 55°. Mark your answer.**

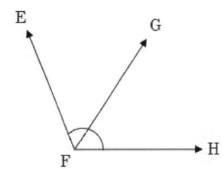

A   100°

B   120°

C   55°

D   110°

Common Core Standard 4.MD.7 – Measurement & Data

☐ **Find the measurement for ∠ KJL if ∠ IJL = 80° and ∠ IJK = 30°. Mark your answer.**

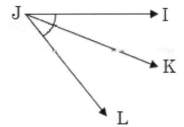

A   50°

B   60°

C   110°

D   30°

Reporting Category 3 – 4.7 (E) Geometry and Measurement

Find the measurement for ∠ ABD if ∠ ABC = 50° and ∠ CBD= 100°. Mark your answer.

A   50°

B   140°

C   100°

D   150°

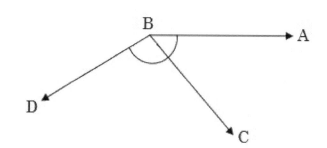

Reporting Category 3 – 4.7 (E) Geometry and Measurement

Find the measurement for ∠ EFG if ∠ EFH = 160° and ∠ GFH = 70°. Mark your answer.

A   160°

B   90°

C   230°

D   80°

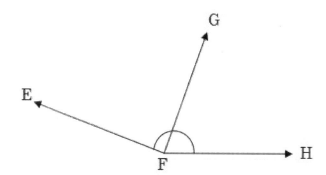

Reporting Category 3 – 4.7 (E) Geometry and Measurement

Find the measurement for ∠ IJL if ∠ IJK = 95° and ∠ KJL = 55°. Mark your answer.

A   40°

B   160°

C   95°

D   150°

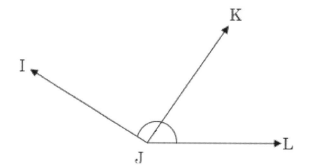

Reporting Category 3 – 4.7 (E) Geometry and Measurement

☐ **Find the measurement for ∠ ABC if ∠ ABD = 120° and ∠ CBD= 60°. Mark your answer.**

A 60°

B 70°

C 120°

D 180°

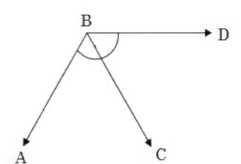

Reporting Category 3 – 4.7 (E) Geometry and Measurement

☐ **Find the measurement for ∠ EFH if ∠ GFH = 35° and ∠ EFG = 45°. Mark your answer.**

A 10°

B 90°

C 80°

D 45°

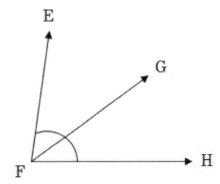

Reporting Category 3 – 4.7 (E) Geometry and Measurement

☐ **Find the measurement for ∠ KJL if ∠ IJL = 140° and ∠ IJK = 75°. Mark your answer.**

A 215°

B 65°

C 70°

D 140°

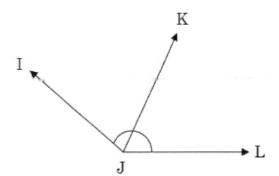

Reporting Category 3 – 4.7 (E) Geometry and Measurement

☐ Find the measurement for ∠ ABD if ∠ ABC = 81° and ∠ CBD= 34°. Mark your answer.

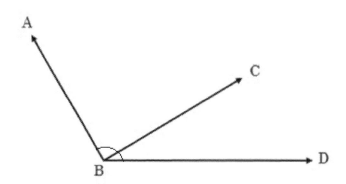

A   110º

B   115º

C   47º

D   81º

Reporting Category 3 – 4.7 (E) Geometry and Measurement

☐ Find the measurement for ∠ GFH if ∠ EFG = 68° and ∠ EFH = 100°. Mark your answer.

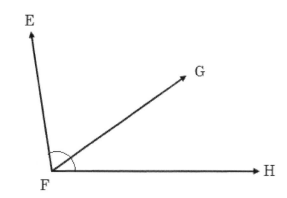

A   100º

B   40º

C   168º

D   32º

Reporting Category 3 – 4.7 (E) Geometry and Measurement

☐ Find the measurement for ∠ IJL if ∠ IJK = 78° and ∠ KJL = 62°. Mark your answer.

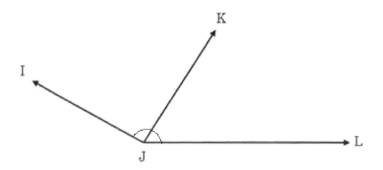

A   140º

B   16º

C   62º

D   150º

Reporting Category 3 – 4.7 (E) Geometry and Measurement

☐ **Find the measurement for ∠ ABC if ∠ ABD = 130° and ∠ CBD= 42°. Mark your answer.**

A   172°

B   90°

C   88°

D   130°

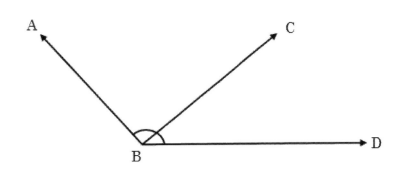

Reporting Category 3 – 4.7 (E) Geometry and Measurement

☐ **Find the measurement for ∠ EFH if ∠ GFH = 37° and ∠ EFG = 113°. Mark your answer.**

A   140°

B   150°

C   113°

D   76°

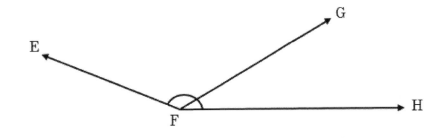

Reporting Category 3 – 4.7 (E) Geometry and Measurement

☐ **Find the measurement for ∠ KJL if ∠ IJL = 135° and ∠ IJK = 95°. Mark your answer.**

A   230°

B   50°

C   95°

D   40°

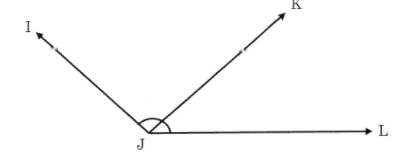

Reporting Category 3 – 4.8 (A) Geometry and Measurement

☐ **What is the best estimate of the weight of an adult rabbit? Mark your answer.**

A   30 pounds

B   30 kilograms

C   30 tons

D   30 ounces

Reporting Category 3 – 4.8 (A) Geometry and Measurement

☐ **Which is the best estimate of the capacity of a bottle of soda? Mark your answer.**

A   2000 cups

B   2000 milliliters

C   2000 quarts

D   2000 gallons

Reporting Category 3 – 4.8 (A) Geometry and Measurement

☐ **Megan read her book for her upcoming homework assignment. She read for 5 hours, how many minutes did Megan read? Mark your answer.**

A   30 minutes

B   300 minutes

C   350 minutes

D   240 minutes

Reporting Category 3 – 4.8 (A) Geometry and Measurement

☐ Eva picked a flower for her mother. Which of the following units would be the most appropriate for measuring the height of the flower? Mark your answer.

A   Liter

B   Kilogram

C   Centimeter

D   Meter

Reporting Category 3 – 4.8 (A) Geometry and Measurement

☐ Joshua is 10 years old, how many months old is Joshua? Mark your answer.

A   10 months

B   120 months

C   100 months

D   110 months

Reporting Category 3 – 4.8 (A) Geometry and Measurement

☐ Which of the following objects would most likely be on the scale if the object weighs 2 ounces? Mark your answer.

A   Bag of oranges

B   Gallon jug of milk

C   Jelly sandwich

D   Car

Reporting Category 3 – 4.8 (A) Geometry and Measurement

Which contain could hold 2 liters of liquid? Mark your answer.

A	B	C	D

Reporting Category 3 – 4.8 (A) Geometry and Measurement

Mr. Campos took his boy scout troop out for a camping trip. They were gone for 5 days. How many hours were the boy scouts gone for? Mark your answer.

A   120 hours

B   60 hours

C   5 hours

D   120 minutes

Reporting Category 3 – 4.8 (A) Geometry and Measurement

Which of the following units would be appropriate for measuring the height of the windmill? Mark your answer.

A   Meter

B   Inch

C   Liter

D   Kilometer

Reporting Category 3 – 4.8 (A) Geometry and Measurement

☐ **Which object could hold one pint of soda? Mark your answer.**

A   B   C   D

Reporting Category 3 – 4.8 (A) Geometry and Measurement

☐ **Kristine is making punch for her party. If she makes 12 pints of punch, how many quarts of punch did she make? Mark your answer.**

A   5 quarts

B   8 quarts

C   12 quarts

D   6 quarts

Reporting Category 3 – 4.8 (A) Geometry and Measurement

☐ **Which of the following units would be the most appropriate for measuring the weight of the boy and girl? Mark your answer.**

A   Ounce

B   Meter

C   Kilogram

D   Millimeter

Name _____

Reporting Category 3 – 4.8 (A) Geometry and Measurement

☐ Kyle read about an animal whose mass was 250 kilograms. Which of the following did Kyle most likely read about? Mark your answer.

A   Adult male deer

B   Adult female dog

C   Adult male lion

D   Adult female horse

Common Core Standard 4.MD.1 – Measurement & Data

☐ Hector's family went on a trip over the weekend. They traveled 80,000 meters on their trip, how many kilometers did they travel? Mark your answer.

A   120 kilometers

B   128 kilometers

C   80 kilometers

D   40 kilometers

Common Core Standard 4.MD.1 – Measurement & Data

☐ Which of the following units would be the most appropriate for measuring the length of a tennis court? Mark your answer.

A   Liter

B   Feet

C   Miles

D   Kilometer

Reporting Category 3 – 4.8 (A) Geometry and Measurement

Which container could have a capacity of 1 pint of ice cream? Mark your answer.

| A | B | C | D |

Reporting Category 3 – 4.8 (A) Geometry and Measurement

Which is the best estimate of the weight of a large sack of potatoes? Mark your answer.

A   5 ounces

B   5 liters

C   5 pounds

D   5 meters

Reporting Category 3 – 4.8 (A) Geometry and Measurement

What is the best estimate of the weight of a bicycle? Mark your answer.

A   8 meters

B   8 ounces

C   8 pounds

D   8 kilometer

Reporting Category 3 – 4.8 (A) Geometry and Measurement

☐ **If the scale shows a weight of 3 grams, which of the objects is most likely to equal 3 grams? Mark your answer.**

A	**B**	**C**	**D**

Reporting Category 3 – 4.8 (A) Geometry and Measurement

☐ **Kesha's pet rabbit and cat weigh exactly the same. Which of the following could the weight of the rabbit and cat? Mark your answer.**

A   50 kilograms

B   6 kilograms

C   100 kilograms

D   75 kilograms

Reporting Category 3 – 4.8 (A) Geometry and Measurement

☐ **What is the best estimate of the weight of a bicycle? Mark your answer.**

A   1 meter

B   1 ounce

C   1 pound

D   1 kilometer

Reporting Category 3 – 4.8 (A) Geometry and Measurement

☐   **Adam's grandmother sent him to the store to buy 2 pounds of apples. Which of the following scales shows the amount of apples he should buy? Mark your answer.**

      A   **B**   **C**   **D**

Reporting Category 3 – 4.8 (A) Geometry and Measurement

☐   **Which object is most likely to have a capacity of 2 gallons? Mark your answer.**

     A   Lake

     B   Container of lemonade

     C   Bottle of medicine

     D   Book

Reporting Category 3 – 4.8 (A) Geometry and Measurement

☐   **Which object is most likely to have a capacity of 2 liters? Mark your answer.**

     A   Washing machine

     B   Shoe

     C   Dose of medicine

     D   Bottle of soda

Reporting Category 3 – 4.8 (B) Geometry and Measurement

☐ The largest recorded bass in Texas was caught at Lake Fork. The bass weighed 18 pounds 14 ounces and was 45 feet 5 inches in length. Which of the following shows the weight of the bass in ounces? Mark your answer.

A   545 ounces

B   82 ounces

C   725 ounces

D   302 ounces

Reporting Category 3 – 4.8 (B) Geometry and Measurement

☐ Lily filled a bottle with 8 quarts of water. Which of the following shows the amount of water in gallons she placed in the bottle? Mark your answer.

A   32 gal

B   2 gal

C   16 gal

D   4 gal

Reporting Category 3 – 4.8 (B) Geometry and Measurement

☐ Ms. Lopez made 3 gallons of lemonade. How many pints of lemonade did she make? Mark your answer.

A   24 pints

B   6 pints

C   12 pints

D   10 pints

Reporting Category 3 – 4.8 (B) Geometry and Measurement

☐ Matthew found a circus poster that was 24 inches wide and 12 inches long. Which of the following represents the perimeter of the poster in feet? Mark your answer.

A   36 ft.

B   72 ft.

C   6 ft.

D   26 ft.

Reporting Category 3 – 4.8 (B) Geometry and Measurement

☐ Mr. Thompson wants to put tile on the floor of his garage. How could he figure how many square feet of tile he needs to buy to complete the job? Mark your answer.

A   240 ÷ 3 ÷ 4

B   240 ÷ 12 × 4

C   240 × 4 × 4

D   240 ÷ 100 ÷ 4

240 in

Reporting Category 3 – 4.8 (B) Geometry and Measurement

☐ Braden's mother bought a bag of apples that weighed 22 ounces. How many pounds of apples did she buy? Mark your answer.

A   22 lbs

B   2 lbs 10 ounces

C   1 lb 16 ounces

D   1 lb 6 ounces

Reporting Category 3 – 4.8 (B) Geometry and Measurement

☐ Allison bought a roll of Christmas wrapping paper that was 4 yards long. What is the length in feet of the wrapping paper? Mark your answer.

A   144 ft.

B   7 ft.

C   12 ft.

D   20 ft.

Reporting Category 3 – 4.8 (B) Geometry and Measurement

☐ A school cafeteria has 48 quarts of orange juice. If they pour the orange juice into gallon jugs, how many gallons will they have? Mark your answer.

A   36 gallons

B   12 gallons

C   24 gallons

D   192 gallons

Reporting Category 3 – 4.8 (B) Geometry and Measurement

☐ The average weight of an adult male African elephant is about 11,000 pounds. About how many tons does the elephant weigh? Mark your answer.

A   1,100 tons

B   550 tons

C   2,000 tons

D $5\frac{1}{2}$ tons

Reporting Category 3 – 4.8 (B) Geometry and Measurement

☐ Which of the following shows how Jose can correctly convert the length of a driveway to inches? Mark your answer.

A   36 ÷ 20

B   20 + 36

C   36 × 20

D   20 × 3

20 yards

Reporting Category 3 – 4.8 (B) Geometry and Measurement

☐ Victoria's mother bought 3 quarts of fruit juice. If a glass holds 1 cup or 8 ounces, how many glasses can she fill with the fruit juice? Mark your answer.

A   12 cups

B   6 cups

C   24 cups

D   3 cups

Reporting Category 3 – 4.8 (B) Geometry and Measurement

☐ Parker weighed 40 pounds when he was 4 years old. How many ounces did he weigh? Mark your answer.

A   160 ounces

B   640 ounces

C   64 ounces

D   440 ounces

Reporting Category 3 – 4.8 (B) Geometry and Measurement

☐ **Mr. Tucker cooked 2 steaks. Mrs. Tucker's steak weighed 8 ounces, and his steak weighed 15 ounces. How many pounds did Mrs. Tucker's steak weigh? Mark your answer.**

A   1 lb. 9 oz.

B $\frac{1}{2}$ lb.

C   1 lb.

D   1 lb. 7 oz.

Reporting Category 3 – 4.8 (B) Geometry and Measurement

☐ **If Mr. Baker needs 50 yards of carpet and he has 142 feet, does he have enough carpet? Mark your answer.**

A   Yes, he will have 42 feet left over.

B   No, he needs 18 more feet.

C   Yes, he has the exact amount he needs.

D   No, he needs 8 more feet.

Reporting Category 3 – 4.8 (B) Geometry and Measurement

☐ **A recipe calls for 4 cups of buttermilk. What is this amount in pints? Mark your answer.**

A   16 pints

B   2 pints

C   8 pints

D   4 pints

Name _____

Reporting Category 3 – 4.8 (B) Geometry and Measurement

☐ The distance from Ethan's house to school is 10,560 feet. How many miles is Ethan's house from school? Mark your answer.

A   1 mile

B   20 miles

C   2 miles

D   4 miles

Reporting Category 3 – 4.8 (B) Geometry and Measurement

☐ If a toy truck weighs 16 ounces, and a ball weighs 5 ounces, how many pounds do the 2 toys weigh altogether? Mark your answer.

A   23 lbs.

B   2 lbs. 5 oz.

C   1 lb. 7 oz.

D   1 lb. 5 oz.

Reporting Category 3 – 4.8 (B) Geometry and Measurement

☐ A snow cone stand bought 2 gallons of cherry syrup. How many pints of cherry syrup did it buy? Mark your answer.

A   8 pints

B   6 pints

C   16 pints

D   12 pints

Reporting Category 3 – 4.8 (B) Geometry and Measurement

☐ **Which has the smallest area in feet? Mark your answer.**

A   A rectangle 24 inches × 12 inches

B   A rectangle 1 foot × 4 feet

C   A square 12 inches × 1 foot

D   A square 2 yards × 2 yards

Reporting Category 3 – 4.8 (B) Geometry and Measurement

☐ **Mr. Sanchez uses 40 feet of waxed paper every week at his store. If he ordered 2 rolls of waxed paper that each contain 250 inches, does he have enough paper to last one week? Mark your answer.**

A   Yes, he has the exact amount he needs.

B   Yes, he will have 20 inches left over.

C   No, he needs 230 more feet of paper.

D   No, he needs 20 more inches of paper.

Reporting Category 3 – 4.8 (B) Geometry and Measurement

☐ **Thomas made 5 quarts of grape drink. How many cups of grape drink did he make? Mark your answer.**

A   10 cups

B   15 cups

C   50 cups

D   20 cups

Reporting Category 3 – 4.8 (B) Geometry and Measurement

☐ An alligator in a zoo weighs 700 pounds 9 ounces. Which of the following shows the weight of the alligator in ounces? Mark your answer.

A   709 ounces

B   11,209 ounces

C   11,309 ounces

D   5,609 ounces

Reporting Category 3 – 4.8 (B) Geometry and Measurement

☐ A store ordered 10 baseball bats that weighed 33 ounces each. How s did the baseball bats weigh altogether? Mark your answer.

A   2 pounds 6 ounces

B   2 pounds 11 ounces

C   20 pounds 6 ounces

D   10 pounds 9 ounces

Reporting Category 3 – 4.8 (B) Geometry and Measurement

☐ A lemonade stand sold 50 cups of lemonade on Saturday. How many gallons of lemonade did the stand sell? Mark your answer.

A   5 gallons

B   12 gallons

C $2\frac{1}{2}$ gallons

D   3 gallons 2 ounces

Reporting Category 3 – 4.8 (C) Geometry and Measurement

Madison saves $3 each week. Which of the following does not represent a total amount she could have saved without having a remainder? Mark your answer.

A $30

B $33

C $27

D $91

Reporting Category 3 – 4.8 (C) Geometry and Measurement

The thermometer shows the temperature of the water in a swimming pool. What temperature is shown below? Mark your answer.

A   81°F

B   82°F

C   83°F

D   100°F

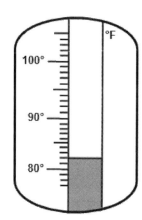

Reporting Category 3 – 4.8 (C) Geometry and Measurement

Betsy's father began mowing the yard at 7:15 this morning. It took him 1 hour 30 minutes to complete the mowing. At what time did he finish mowing? Mark your answer.

A   3:35 PM

B   7:45 AM

C   8:45 AM

D   9:30 AM

Reporting Category 3 – 4.8 (C) Geometry and Measurement

☐ A fast moving cold front came through Plano yesterday morning. If the thermometer shows the temperature when the cold front came through, what was the temperature by noon if it dropped by 19°? Mark your answer.

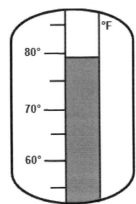

A   89°F

B   61°F

C   79°F

D   60°F

Reporting Category 3 – 4.8 (C) Geometry and Measurement

☐ Phillip received all nickels in change from a purchase at a convenience store. Which of the following amounts of money could not be the total amount of change he received? Mark your answer.

A $0.60

B $0.90

C $0.27

D $0.35

Reporting Category 3 – 4.8 (C) Geometry and Measurement

☐ Josiah watches his favorite video on Saturday afternoons. It lasts 3 hours. How many minutes does it take for him to watch the video? Mark your answer.

A   120 min

B   180 min

C   60 min

D   160 min

Reporting Category 3 – 4.8 (C) Geometry and Measurement

☐ Cameron did his chores in 1 hour 53 minutes. His sister did her chores in 125 minutes. How much less time did Cameron spend on his chores than his sister? Mark your answer.

A   237 min

B   12 min

C   73 min

D   65 min

Reporting Category 3 – 4.8 (C) Geometry and Measurement

☐ Glenn had $0.25. His mother gave him 2 dimes and 3 nickels for his allowance. How much the total amount of money does Glenn have? Mark your answer.

A $0.75

B $0.60

C $0.65

D $0.85

Reporting Category 3 – 4.8 (C) Geometry and Measurement

☐ The thermometer below shows Monday's temperature. If it was 18°C warmer on Saturday, what was Saturday's temperature? Mark your answer.

A   2°C

B   48°C

C   38°C

D   21°C

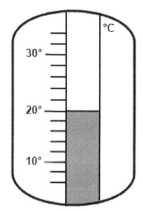

Name _____

☐ Dylan ran in a race at school. His time to reach the finish line was 45 seconds. If Samuel ran in the same race, and his time was 54 seconds, how many seconds did Dylan finish ahead of Samuel? Mark your answer.

A   99 sec

B   11 sec

C   9 sec

D   19 sec

☐ Sarah had $.0.60. She let Marcy borrow $0.34 to buy a piece of candy. Which coins would show much money Sarah has left? Mark your answer.

A   Three quarters, three nickels, and four pennies

B   One quarter and one penny

C   One quarter, one dime, and one penny

D   Three dimes and fives pennies

☐ The temperature at noon was 65°F. By 3 o'clock that afternoon, the temperature had risen 20°. What was the temperature at 3 o'clock? Mark your answer.

A   85°F

B   80°F

C   75°F

D   40°F

Name _____

Reporting Category 4 – 4.9 (A) Data Analysis

☐ **Henry kept track of his height since he was born. Look at the line plot below and find the correct answer to the questions below.**

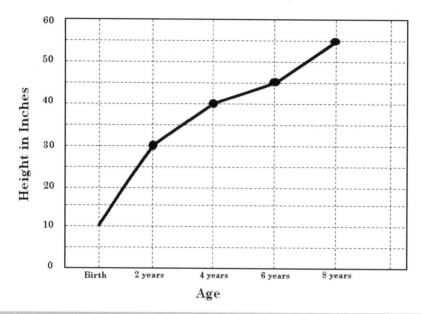

☐ **How tall was Henry when he was four years old? Mark your answer.**

A	30 inches	C	45 inches
B	40 inches	D	35 inches

☐ **How tall might be Henry at 10 years old? Mark your answer.**

A	65 inches	C	50 inches
B	55 inches	D	85 inches

☐ **How old was Henry when he was 30 inches tall? Mark your answer.**

A	3 years old	C	4 years old
B	5 years old	D	2 years old

Name _____

Reporting Category 4 – 4.9 (A) Data Analysis

☐ The daily temperatures were tracked for Dallas last week and recorded on the line graph below. Use the graph to find the correct answer to the questions below.

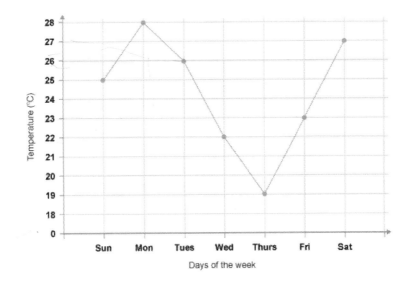

☐ Which day experienced the highest temperature for the week? Mark your answer.

A   Thursday   C   Monday

B   Saturday   D   Sunday

☐ What was the difference in temperature from Tuesday to Friday? Mark your answer.

A   5 degrees difference   C   4 degrees difference

B   3 degrees difference   D   2 degrees difference

☐ What was the temperature for Wednesday? Mark your answer.

A   20°   C   19°

B   22°   D   18°

Reporting Category 4 – 4.9 (A) Data Analysis

Becky loves the World Cup and decided to track the number of goals scored in each game of her favority team. Use the plot below to find the correct answer to the questions.

Each x = 1 goal scored

Game Number

How many goals did Becky's team score in Game 3 and Game 6? Mark your answer.

A   Ten

B   Eleven

C   Nine

D   Eight

Which game did Becky's team score exactly one goal? Mark your answer.

A   Game 6

B   Game 2

C   Game 4

D   Game 1

What is the difference in the amount of goals scored in Game 1 versus Game 6? Mark your answer.

A   2 goals

B   1 goal

C   4 goals

D   3 goals

Reporting Category 4 – 4.9 (A) Data Analysis

☐ **Mr. Reddy gave his classroom a math test on Friday. He was very happy to see that his class did well on the test. Use the plot below to find the correct answer to the questions.**

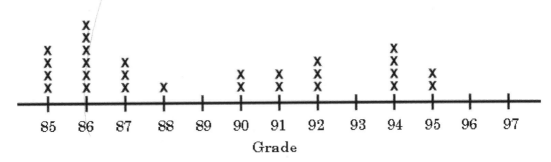

Math Test Scores

Grade

☐ **How many received a grade of 91 on their math test? Mark your answer.**

A   Three

B   Four

C   Two

D   Five

☐ **What was the highest grade received by the students on the test? Mark your answer.**

A   97

B   95

C   96

D   85

☐ **How many students scored less than a 90 on the math test? Mark your answer.**

A   15 students

B   13 students

C   14 students

D   12 students

Reporting Category 4 – 4.9 (B) Data Analysis

☐ The graphs below show the amount of rain and temperatures during May for some cities in Texas. Which city had less than 4 inches of rain and a temperature greater than 71°? Mark your answer.

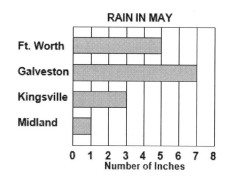

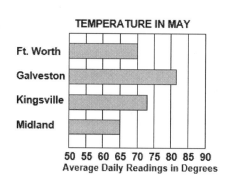

A   Midland   C   Galveston

B   Ft. Worth   D   Kingsville

Reporting Category 4 – 4.9 (B) Data Analysis

☐ Jack's class has 29 students. His class wanted to find out which was the favorite meat served by the cafeteria. The graph shows the results of the survey. Which of the following statements is a correct conclusion from the graph? Mark your answer.

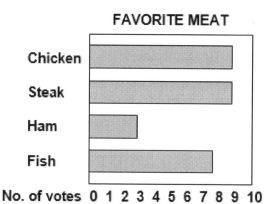

A   More students liked ham than steak.

B   About the same number liked steak as liked chicken.

C   Fish is the most popular meat.

D   Ham was chosen twice as many times as fish.

Reporting Category 4 – 4.9 (B) Data Analysis

☐ The graph shows the results of a survey to determine the favorite vegetable of customers at Bailey's Cafeteria. What was the total number of votes on the 3 vegetables that received the greatest number of votes? Mark your answer.

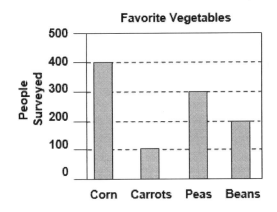

A   1000   C   600

B   900   D   800

Reporting Category 4 – 4.9 (B) Data Analysis

☐ The graph shows the number of cars washed at a car wash in four weeks. If the car wash earned $7 per car, how much money did the car wash earn during Week 2? Mark your answer.

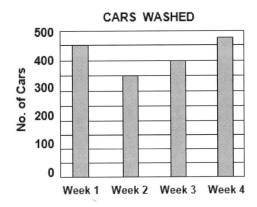

A $2450

B $2800

C $2150

D $357

Reporting Category 4 – 4.9 (B) Data Analysis

☐ **Mr. Owen's sailboat is on Lake Martin and traveling toward the shore. The graph below shows how the distance to the shore changes. At what time will Mr. Owen reach the shore if he keeps going at the same rate? Mark your answer.**

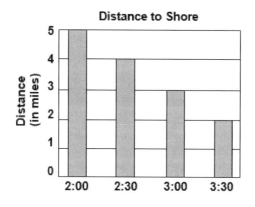

A	4:00	**C**	5:00
B	5:30	**D**	4:30

Reporting Category 4 – 4.9 (B) Data Analysis

☐ **A candy store kept a record of the amount of candy sold during one week. The graph shows the candy sales. If the candy was priced at $3 a pound, how much money did the candy store earn on Friday? Mark your answer.**

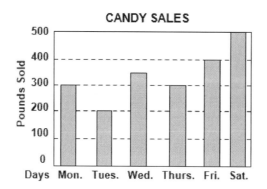

A	$900	**C**	$600
B	$1600	**D**	$1200

Reporting Category 4 – 4.9 (B) Data Analysis

☐ The graph shows the different kinds of trees found in a city park. The total number of willow and pine trees is the same as the total number of _____. Mark your answer.

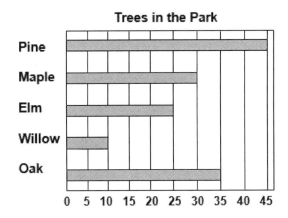

A   pine and elm trees   C   oak and maple trees

B   maple and elm trees   D   maple and willow trees

Reporting Category 4 – 4.9 (B) Data Analysis

☐ The graph shows how the students in Mr. Baylor's class voted when asked to choose their favorite subject. How many students voted for math? Mark your answer.

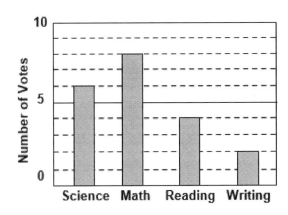

A   10   C   8

B   7   D   9

Reporting Category 4 – 4.9 (B) Data Analysis

☐ The graphs show items sold by fourth grade students and the amount they earned. Which item sold 50 and earned about $265? Mark your answer.

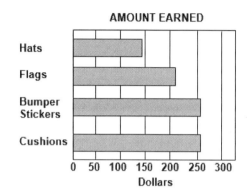
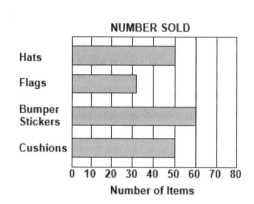

A   Hats

B   Flags

C   Cushions

D   Bumper stickers

Reporting Category 4 – 4.9 (B) Data Analysis

☐ The graph below shows the width of some of the world's largest flowers. Based on the information in the graph, which statement appears to be true? Mark your answer.

A   The Brazilian Dutchman's Pipe is twice as wide as the Magnolia.

B   The Sunflower is about 22 centimeters wider than the Magnolia.

C   The Giant Water Lily and the Sunflower are the same width.

D   The Brazilian Dutchman's Pipe Is 35 centimeters tall.

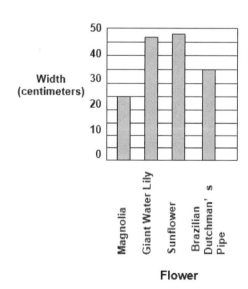

Reporting Category 4 – 4.9 (B) Data Analysis

☐ Destiny recorded the following amounts of rainfall for one 4-day period. According to the graph, how much more rain fell on Wednesday than on Monday? Mark your answer.

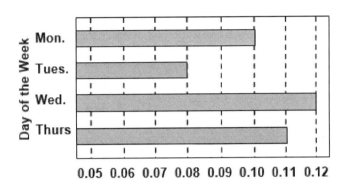

A   0.20 in.   C   0.04 in.

B   0.22 in.   D   0.02 in.

Reporting Category 4 – 4.9 (B) Data Analysis

☐ The graph shows how much money two girls spent. According to the graph, what was the total amount of money the girls spent on items that cost less than $5? Mark your answer.

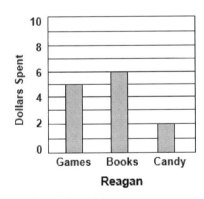
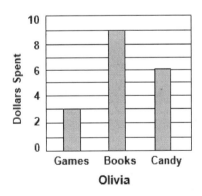

A $10   C $5

B $6   D $31

Name _____

Reporting Category 4 – 4.9 (B) Data Analysis

☐ The graph shows the favorite colors of some fourth grade students. How many more students chose yellow and blue than green and blue? Mark your answer.

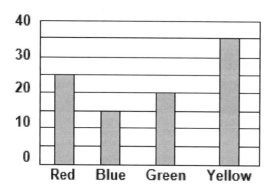

A   25   C   5

B   15   D   10

Reporting Category 4 – 4.9 (B) Data Analysis

☐ The graph shows the number of cookies a bakery sold in one week. Mrs. Norris bought all of the chocolate chip cookies for a party. If 10 guests were invited to the party, how many cookies could each guest eat if the cookies were divided equally among the guests? Mark your answer.

A   2

B   3

C   8

D   4

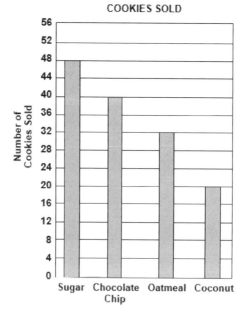

Reporting Category 4 – 4.9 (B) Data Analysis

☐ **Each hour Mr. Long counted the number of customers who ate lunch in his restaurant. If each customer spent at least $5, what is the least amount of money Mr. Long earned at 12:00? Mark your answer.**

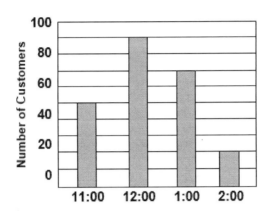

A	$425	C	$4500
B	$450	D	$45

Reporting Category 4 – 4.9 (B) Data Analysis

☐ **The graph shows the number of tickets four students sold for a raffle. How many more tickets did Victor sell than Zoe? Mark your answer.**

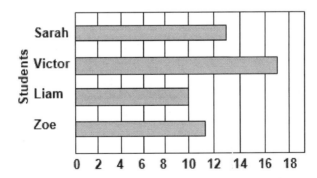

A	6	C	8
B	28	D	7

4.2 (A)
Page 1 .... B, B, B
Page 2 .... A, B, C
Page 3 .... D, A, C
Page 4 .... B, A, C

4.2 (B)
Page 5 .... A, D, B
Page 6 .... D, C, B
Page 7 .... B, D, C
Page 8 .... C, D, A
Page 9 .... A, D, C
Page 10 .... C, D, B
Page 11 .... A, B, C
Page 12 .... C, D, B

4.2 (C)
Page 13 .... B, D, B
Page 14 .... A, C, D
Page 15 .... C, A, D
Page 16 .... A, C, D
Page 17 .... C, B, D
Page 18 .... B, C, A

4.2 (D)
Page 19 .... D, D, C
Page 20 .... C, A
Page 21 .... A, D, D
Page 22 .... D, C
Page 23 .... D, B, A
Page 24 .... B, A

Page 25 .... B, D, D
Page 26 .... B, C

4.2 (E)
Page 27 .... B, A, C
Page 28 .... C, B, C
Page 29 .... D, A, C
Page 30 .... B, B, D
Page 31 .... D, C, A
Page 32 .... A, D, D
Page 33 .... B, D, C
Page 34 .... D, A, D

4.2 (F)
Page 35 .... A, D, D
Page 36 .... A, C, B
Page 37 .... C, D, A
Page 38 .... C, B, A

4.2 (G)
Page 39 .... B, A, B
Page 40 .... C, D, C
Page 41 .... C, C, B
Page 42 .... C, B, D

4.2 (H)
Page 43 .... B, C, B
Page 44 .... D, C, D
Page 45 .... D, C, B
Page 46 .... C, B, A

4.3 (A)

Page 47 ………. D, B, B

Page 48 ………. C, A, C

Page 49 ………. B, C, C

Page 50 ………. B, C, A

4.3 (B)

Page 51 ………. B, D, D

Page 52 ………. C, B, B

Page 53 ………. D, B, A

Page 54 ………. D, C, C

4.3 (C)

Page 55 ………. A, C, D

Page 56 ………. C, C, B

Page 57 ………. B, C, A

Page 58 ………. D, D, C

4.3 (D)

Page 59 ………. D, C, D

Page 60 ………. C, B, B

Page 61 ………. A, D, B

Page 62 ………. C, D, D

4.3 (H)

Page 63 ………. D, D, B

Page 64 ………. B, C, D

Page 65 ………. A, D, C

Page 66 ………. D, B, D

4.3 (E)

Page 67 ………. B, A, C

Page 68 ………. D, B, C

Page 69 ………. D, D, C

Page 70 ………. C, B, B

Page 71 ………. D, B, B

Page 72 ………. C, A, D

Page 73 ………. C, B, D

Page 74 ………. B, C, A

4.3 (F)

Page 75 ………. B, B, A

Page 76 ………. C, D, A

Page 77 ………. B, D, A

Page 78 ………. C, D, A

Page 79 ………. A, B, A

Page 80 ………. D, A, D

Page 81 ………. C, B, D

Page 82 ………. A, D, C

4.4 (A)

Page 83 ………. C, D, B

Page 84 ………. C, C, D

Page 85 ………. B, D, B

Page 86 ………. A, B, D

Page 87 ………. B, D, B

Page 88 ………. D, A, A

Page 89 ………. B, A, D

Page 90 ………. A, D, C

4.4 (B)

Page 91 .... D, C, B
Page 92 .... C, D, D
Page 93 .... D, C, B
Page 94 .... D, A, C

4.4 (C)

Page 95 .... C, C, D
Page 96 .... B, B
Page 97 .... D
Page 98 .... B, C, A
Page 99 .... D, D
Page 100 .... C, B, D
Page 101 .... D, C, B
Page 102 .... A, C

4.4 (D)

Page 103 .... D, B, C
Page 104 .... B, D, C
Page 105 .... D, A, B
Page 106 .... A, A, C
Page 107 .... C, C, B
Page 108 .... B, B, B
Page 109 .... A, B, B
Page 110 .... A, D, C

4.4 (E)

Page 111 .... C, D, C
Page 112 .... B, D, B
Page 113 .... D, B, B
Page 114 .... C, B, C

4.4 (F)

Page 115 .... B, D, C
Page 116 .... C, D, A
Page 117 .... A, A, B
Page 118 .... A, C, B
Page 119 .... B, D, B
Page 120 .... D, C, C
Page 121 .... B, C, B
Page 122 .... D, C, C

4.4 (G)

Page 123 .... C, B, D
Page 124 .... C, A, C
Page 125 .... B, A, B
Page 126 .... A, A, C

4.4 (H)

Page 127 .... C, D, B
Page 128 .... B, C, D
Page 129 .... A, A, C
Page 130 .... A, A, A

3.5 (A)

Page 131 .... C, D, B
Page 132 .... B, A, D
Page 133 .... C, C, A

4.5 (B)

Page 134 .... B, D
Page 135 .... C, B
Page 136 .... D, B
Page 137 .... C, D

Page 138 .... C, C	**Page 161** .... B, B
Page 139 .... D, D	**Page 162** .... B, D, C
Page 140 .... D, B	**Page 163** .... B, A
Page 141 .... C, C	**Page 164** .... C, A, A
	Page 165 .... B, C

4.5(D)

4.6 (D)

Page 142 .... C, B, B	**Page 166** .... B, D, B
Page 143 .... D, B, C	**Page 167** .... B, D, B
Page 144 .... A, D, D	**Page 168** .... B, D, B
Page 145 .... A, C, A	**Page 169** .... B, D, C

4.6 (A)

4.7 (C)

Page 146 .... C, B, A	**Page 170** .... C, A, D
Page 147 .... C, D, D	**Page 171** .... B, D, C
Page 148 .... A, A, C	**Page 172** .... A, B, C
Page 149 .... B, C, D	**Page 173** .... A, D, C
	Page 174 .... C, A, B
	Page 175 .... A, C, B

4.6 (B)

Page 150 .... C, C, D	**Page 176** .... D, B, C
Page 151 .... B, B, D	**Page 177** .... D, C, A
Page 152 .... A, D, C	
Page 153 .... B, B, C	
Page 154 .... A, D, C	**4.7 (D)**
Page 155 .... C, B, C	**Page 178** .... OPEN, OPEN, OPEN
Page 156 .... B, C, D	**Page 179** .... OPEN, OPEN, OPEN
Page 157 .... C, D, B	**Page 180** .... OPEN, OPEN, OPEN
	Page 181 .... OPEN, OPEN, OPEN
	Page 182 .... OPEN, OPEN, OPEN
4.6 (C)	**Page 183** .... OPEN, OPEN, OPEN
Page 158 .... D, C, B	**Page 184** .... OPEN, OPEN, OPEN
Page 159 .... C, B	**Page 185** .... OPEN, OPEN, OPEN
Page 160 .... A, C, C	

4.7 (E)

Page 186 .... B, C, D
Page 187 .... C, A, D
Page 188 .... A, C, D
Page 189 .... C, D, A
Page 190 .... D, B, D
Page 191 .... A. C. B
Page 192 .... B, D, A
Page 193 .... C, B, D

4.8 (A)

Page 194 .... D, B, B
Page 195 .... C, B, C
Page 196 .... D, A, A
Page 197 .... B, D, C
Page 198 .... C, B, B
Page 199 .... D, C, C
Page 200 .... C, B, C
Page 201 .... B, B, D

4.8 (B)

Page 202 .... D, B, A
Page 203 .... C, B, D
Page 204 .... C, B, D
Page 205 .... C, A, B
Page 206 .... B, D, B
Page 207 .... C, D, C
Page 208 .... C, B, D
Page 209 .... B, C, D

4.8 (C)

Page 210 .... D, B, C
Page 211 .... D, C, B
Page 212 .... B, B, C
Page 213 .... C, B, A

4.9 (A)

Page 214 .... B, A, D
Page 215 .... C, B, B
Page 216 .... A, B, D
Page 217 .... C, B, C

4.9(B)

Page 218 .... D, B
Page 219 .... B, A
Page 220 .... D, D
Page 221 .... B, C
Page 222 .... C, D
Page 223 .... D, C
Page 224 .... B, D
Page 225 .... B, A

Made in the USA
Lexington, KY
24 May 2017